Reading this book has been a great way to validate what we are already doing as well as giving a lot of new ideas about what we could be doing next!

Jan Strang
Head of Retail Finance
Nordea Bank

An enlightening fact-based read that provides direction without forcing a solution to what is arguably the biggest challenge faced by businesses today, digital transformation.

Paul O'Leary
Managing Director, UK
IKANO Bank

The challenges overcome by global banks of different nature and size provide readers with a useful tool to be able to embrace innovation themselves.

Alberto Greppi
Head of Investment Team, Neva Finventures
Intesa Sanpaolo

If you work with banks, or in banking, this is a must read crash course in the best practices of their varying innovation models.

Will Mason
Director of Markets and Innovation
Experian

These case studies demonstrate that whilst there are many paths to success, banks need to focus as much on how they approach innovation as what they hope to deliver in order to make a lasting transformation.

Anthony Craufurd
Venture and Startup Engagement Director
VISA Europe

This book shows that there is no silver bullet when it comes to how to drive innovation within companies, it is difficult to innovate within an established corporate culture, flexibility is key and the ability to pivot quickly if needed.

Werner Decker
EVP/GM, Global Merchant Services International
American Express

The success levers and learnings from each case study are very clearly laid out. What I really love about it is that it is practical, actionable and easy to absorb.

Pinar Alpay
Senior Vice President, Global Payment Solutions & Transformation
FIS

Christer's case studies are a valuable resource for operators attempting to drive change in and around financial institutions.

Philip Bodell
Corporate Development Director
Fiserv

Transactional to Transformational

Transactional to Transformational

How Banks Innovate

By Christer Holloman

WILEY

Library of Congress Cataloging-in-Publication Data is Available:

ISBN 978-1-119-79128-7 (hardback)
ISBN 978-1-119-79132-4 (ePub)
ISBN 978-1-119-79129-4 (ePDF)

Cover Design: Wiley
Cover Image: © Liu zishan/Shutterstocks

Set in 11.5/14pt STIXTwoText by Straive, Chennai, India

10 9 8 7 6 5 4 3 2 1

Conor

Thank you for your support throughout this process

You are destined for greatness

Contents

Foreword

O ver their lifetime, banks have not been known for innovation. They have long held a privileged position of trust
in society, as safeguards of our wealth and most private
information. As such, customers have traditionally been happy
with low rates of innovation, with almost 80% of us actively
choosing to remain with the big traditional banks, despite financial
incentive and regulatory support to switch. This was because, in
the old world, we had accepted that security and innovation were
an insurmountable trade-off and that when given the choice,
we would rather that our bank kept our money safe than give us
more innovative technologies.

As you know very well if you are reading this book, this is no
longer true. Following a perfect storm of events that shook both the
industry players as well as the expectations of bank customers, we
are now living in an age where banks have to compare themselves
to, and collaborate with, small fintech and large tech companies in
the race to satisfy their customers' needs.

In the events that led to this dramatic change in the banking industry, the 2008 global financial crisis has been considered a cornerstone. The crush of incumbent firms and the banking system led to the loss of customer trust, and the ripples of this shock continued for people who experienced financial losses in the crisis and the following economic downturn. Even though most big banks remained a safe place in people's eyes for keeping their financial assets, lack of transparency and persistent high fees caused a different kind of trust problem that banks needed to solve.

Another driver of the transformation of banks into innovative organisations has been their realisation of the different needs and habits of 'millennials' who are starting to become their customers. The differences in this generation's life goals, spending habits and employment patterns from previous generations are stark enough to make any organisation stop and think about reconfiguring their product portfolio. With lower home ownership rates, high student debt, variable employment and income, low trust in established institutions and, perhaps most importantly, high willingness to share their data for better services, millennials require not only a different set of financial services but also a much more data-driven, personalised approach to their finances.

Finally, we must mention the buzz word, open banking, if we are to discuss innovation in banking. Open banking is a set of regulations that has been positioned as the catalyst for reinvention within the banking sector. Starting with the UK and EU in 2018, versions of open banking regulation are spreading fast around the world, with noteworthy examples in Australia, Brazil, Canada, India and Singapore. In a nutshell, open banking facilitates competition by mandating incumbent banks to produce open access to valuable current account and other financial data via application programming interfaces (APIs) to trusted third party providers. In other words, it gives customers control over their financial data and allows data-driven new entrants to access the data they need in order to compete with big banks. Open banking has spurred competition to big banks, not only from small innovative fintechs but also from BigTech. Using the new regulations to access customers' bank data, the likes of Amazon, Google and Facebook are taking big strides into banking as I write this. Examples include Amazon's extension of credit to businesses on its platform via Amazon Lending, Facebook's aggressive implementation of P2P payments into its social platform and Google's announcement of basic banking (e.g. checking account) services starting in the US in 2021.

Against this backdrop, Christer Holloman's book on how banks innovate is both important and timely. Banks need to innovate in order to stay alive. However, it is not necessarily easy for them to do so given their legacy systems and safety-focused culture. In this book, Christer provides an array of innovation efforts by top banks around the world. What I find particularly noteworthy here is the honest approach to the problems faced by these vast institutions. There is no magic pill for banks to become data-driven technology organisations overnight; innovation takes constant effort and change in management. For those organisations that are at the start of this journey, Christer's book provides an open buffet of innovation efforts from the industry to consider and implement. These insights are not only valuable to other banks that are realising the need to start an aggressive innovation programme, but also to any big organisations that are being disrupted by data-driven technology organisations.

Pinar Ozcan
Professor of Entrepreneurship & Innovation
Saïd Business School, University of Oxford

Introduction

I n 2016 Goldman launched the digital bank Marcus to diversify its revenue and funding sources by offering savings accounts and personal loans to retail customers. Within 6 months of launch they had signed up over 200,000 customers and taken in more than $6 billion in deposits. In 2019, after 3 years of preparation and a $250 million investment, Royal Bank of Scotland launched its digital bank called Bó. Six months later RBS declared the initiative a failure and closed it down.

Why is it that some banks are better at innovating than others?

That is the exact question I have been asking myself since 2014 when I founded Divido, a software platform today used by some of the largest banks in the world such as HSBC, BNP and ING to offer 'Buy Now, Pay Later' finance to retailers and consumers. As an SaaS platform, charging a transaction fee, I realised early on that we would only be successful if the banks were successful in launching and scaling this new proposition. The quicker the better. In addition to the clients of Divido, from which I have had the opportunity to learn best practices first hand, I have met with 100+ banks over the years and whenever I got the chance I would ask, 'How do you innovate? What has worked, what has not, and why?' What began as a quest to set my own business up for success has evolved into a repeatable blueprint that has been shared, used and validated by a diverse set of banks: big and small, long established and brand new, from the west and the east. It was when I was discussing these insights at a workshop with a bank last year that their CEO suggested I should write a book about how banks innovate.

Banks, like any business, need to defend and grow their market share. That can only happen through innovation, which for a lot of banks means moving away from being a processor of transactions. That said, just because a bank once did something innovative, it does not mean they are an innovative bank. Just because they churn out press releases announcing innovations, it does not mean the innovation was any good or that they are good at innovating. Several of the banks I have worked with to launch 'Buy Now, Pay Later' told me that it was their first new product at this scale in over 10 years. It is hard to get good at something when you do not do it very often. All the more reason to make sure you do your homework and prepare to make sure you get it right the first time when you do decide to innovate. For some bank executives, delivering an innovation can make or break their career. Even those who innovate more often say that everything tends to take longer than they like, costs more than they had budgeted for and the end result does not transform the bank or excite the end-users. In conclusion, there seems to be room for improvement all around.

Through a series of case studies you are invited to meet and learn first-hand from the people and teams that have delivered a number of very different innovations successfully across a diverse group of banks. Banks featured include: Bank of America, BBVA, Citi, Crédit Agricole, Danske Bank, Deutsche Bank, ING, J.P. Morgan, Lloyds Bank, Metro Bank, N26, National Australia Bank, Royal Bank of Canada, Santander, Standard Chartered and Swedbank.

If you are looking for a silver bullet, you have come to the wrong place. This book will, however, equip you with ideas, tools and actionable hands-on advice to challenge, inform and validate your own thinking. You will learn how these particular banks delivered new solutions to consumers and businesses, products as well as services, across the spectrum of buy, build and partner. There is even a bonus section talking about changing ways of working, creating a better foundation for enabling innovation in the first place. The banks have been chosen based on their size, location and type of innovation to give you the broadest breadth of reference points.

Whilst a lot of care has been taken to ensure consistency in detail across all chapters, you will notice slight variations because different banks were comfortable sharing different information. I have done my best to tease out the learnings for you, but in cases where it is not as obvious, I challenge you to read between the lines. If you want to dig deeper into any specific case, there are over 100 hours of additional interview material that I could not fit in the book, so register on www.howbanksinnovate.com to access more material from the banks featured, with full-length interviews and videos.

If you have a successful innovation case you think we should profile on our website and share with our community, get in touch via www.howbanksinnovate.com.

Christer Holloman

Part I
Buy

Chapter 1
Lloyds Banking Group Investing from the Balance Sheet

Case: Thought Machine

Executive Summary

In 2018, Lloyds Banking Group (LBG) announced the next three-year phase of their strategy, designed to set the group up for success in a digital world. In establishing the activities to deliver this strategy, they recognised the potential of investing in fintechs using their balance sheet to accelerate their own transformation and even to unlock new business model opportunities.

They recognised that in order to realise this opportunity they would need to develop the Group's partnering capabilities; for example, creating a shared approach to pipeline development, getting the right tooling in place and building a group-wide narrative around it. A particular critical part was determining the correct partnership structure for each opportunity.

To deliver their ambition they mobilised innovation working groups in each major part of the Group alongside a central fintech team. Together, these groups adopted a shared language and approach for pipeline management. Whilst this went some way to mobilising their pipeline, this consistent view also allowed them to identify common bottlenecks, which they needed to address to make the aggregate pipeline more robust.

Lloyds also used key pathfinder opportunities, such as their partnership with Thought Machine, to develop, surface and agree some important principles at more advanced stages of their pipeline. This included their equity investment rationale. Here they established two main principles: firstly, to only make investments where they expected to sustain a strategic relationship with a fintech; secondly, they required a clear articulation of the necessary strategic benefits of investment relative to what could be achieved through a commercial contract alone.

Whilst the bank acknowledges that it has more to learn and develop with regards to how to best invest in fintechs, the early results have been positive. Their capabilities in emerging technologies have been significantly advanced through this approach and several new customer services have been launched.

Introductions

Do you want more details about this case? Find additional highlights from these interviews at www.howbanksinnovate.com.

Juan Gomez Reino, Group Chief Technology Officer

Juan has been the Chief Technology Officer for LBG since 2019. Juan joined LBG in November 2014, initially as the COO for Consumer Finance before moving into the Insurance division in May 2016 as Transformation Director. Prior to joining the Group, Juan held a number of senior roles at Santander UK and Banco Santander, latterly reporting to the CRO and COO with responsibility for balance sheet management, liquidity, funds transfer pricing and asset-backed funding. Juan graduated from the International School of Economics Rotterdam in 1994 (BA in Economics and Business Administration), has an MSc in Finance from Universidad Autónoma de Madrid and a BSc in Mathematics from UNED. He is also an alumnus of Stanford University's Graduate School of Business.

Carla Antunes da Silva, Group Strategy Director

Since joining LBG in October 2015, Carla has led the work on the 2018–2020 Group Strategic Review and, prior to that, the work on the Bank of the Future, which served as the backdrop to the market announcement. She and her teams are responsible for supporting senior management with strategic decisions made at both the Group and Business Unit level and making recommendations to the Group on all areas of major strategic significance, such as mergers, acquisitions/disposals, joint ventures and partnerships. They manage the Group's relationships with shareholders, the analyst community and the wider investment community, and provide coverage of Group-wide competitor analysis, which drives strategic decision-making through insightful analysis of the industry and competitors.

Zak Mian, Group Transformation Director

Zak joined the Group in 1989 as a Business Analyst in IT. He is now Group Director for the Transformation division and is responsible for group-wide Transformation and strategic change programmes across all their business areas and functions. Before his current appointment Zak was responsible for the Group's Digital Transformation and End-to-End Journey Transformation agenda, leading the strategic direction for digitising the front- and back-end of the bank to deliver market-leading customer propositions. Prior to this, he was Retail CIO for Lloyds UK Retail Banking for over three years.

Background

Key Figures

Total assets: £900 billion
Number of customers: 30 million
Number of branches: 2,000
Number of employees: 60,000
(Approximate as of 2020)

LBG is one of the largest financial services groups in the UK, providing a wide range of banking and financial services, focused on personal and commercial customers.

The Group's main business activities are retail, commercial and corporate banking, general insurance, and life, pensions and investment provision. Services are offered through a number of brands including Lloyds Bank, Halifax, Bank of Scotland and Scottish Widows, and a range of distribution channels. This includes the largest branch network in the UK and a comprehensive digital, telephony and mobile services.

Since 2018, LBG has had their strategic priorities focused on the financial needs and behaviours of the customer of the future and they break it down into four themes:

- **Leading customer experience.** In order to be the best bank for customers, they recognise that they must continue to adapt to changes in customer behaviour, technology-driven competition and regulation. Their propositions must be reflective of heightened customer expectations for ease of access, personalisation and relevance, as well as the needs created by changing life patterns. In September 2020, their digital bank had 17.1 million active users.
- **Digitising the group.** Their cost position and customer franchise are sources of competitive advantage. However, they are not complacent and realise they must further digitise the group to drive additional operational efficiencies, improve the experience of their customers and colleagues and allow them

to invest more for the future. In addition, they must continue to simplify and progressively transform their IT architecture in order to use data more efficiently, enhance their multichannel customer engagement and create a scalable and resilient infrastructure.

- **Maximising the group's capabilities.** To better address their customers' banking and insurance needs as an integrated financial services provider and improve their overall experience, they want to make better use of their competitive strengths and unique business model.
- **Transforming their ways of working.** Their colleagues are crucial to the success of their business. In order to deliver their transformation during the current strategic plan and beyond, their colleagues will require new skills and capabilities to reflect the changing needs of the business as it adapts to the evolving operating environment. At the same time, colleague expectations of their employers are changing. As a result, they are making their biggest ever investment in colleagues to ensure that they continue to attract, develop and retain these skills and capabilities, while fostering a culture that supports a way of working that is agile, trust-based and reinforces the group's values.

To deliver this ambitious transformation, LBG increased its strategic investment to more than £3 billion over the plan period.

Problem

LBG aimed to deliver this transformation agenda whilst maintaining their cost-to-income ratio. As such, the group recognised the importance of utilising every available transformation lever.

Internally, the group brought the end-to-end change functions into a single area called Group Transformation. The function was organised into value streams aligned to customer journeys and an increasing amount of change began to be delivered using agile principles and practices. Additional transformation enablers such as Design and Data Science were also scaled up with the aim of delivering more customer-focused change, whilst lowering the overall cost of change.

However, as they looked across the industry, there was an external lever that other banks appeared to be increasingly using that did not play a big role in their change and innovation toolkit at the time: working closer with fintechs.

They saw a lot of examples of banks and insurers announcing either direct partnerships or investments. Within Lloyds, the Group had interacted with the fintech ecosystem through various industry initiatives or incubators but without any material commercial outcomes, so they set out to understand the opportunity better. Firstly, could fintech partnering be a relevant delivery route for innovation across LBG? Secondly, if it could, then why had it not emerged organically to date?

By mapping external innovation activity against LBG's strategic agenda, they found sufficient evidence to support two delivery goals. Firstly, the opportunity to accelerate or enhance their technology transformation agenda, especially where that leveraged emerging technologies. Secondly, the opportunity to ensure they were able to provide best-in-class products and services to their customers, especially where this stretched beyond traditional balance sheet products.

On the second point, they found evidence of several friction points that collectively pointed to the need to develop a specialist set of capabilities, processes and culture in order to enable them to fully benefit from this opportunity. They needed to enhance the 'rails' on which partnering opportunities could run, meaning the journey right from opportunity identification through to execution. For example:

- There was no consistent way of monitoring or segmenting the fintech landscape to support opportunity identification.
- There was no consistent approach to help to surface business needs that would benefit most from partnering solutions.

- Some elements of their policies added out-sized friction to conducting proofs of concept with third parties.
- In some places their technology capabilities made integration with third parties more challenging.
- There were few established routes through which to surface promising innovation partnering opportunities to an adequate level.
- There was no existing framework for considering strategic investments in partners at this scale.
- Their traditional corporate development activity had focused on relatively large-scale acquisitions and disposals, where the value was primarily in the existing balance sheet as opposed to a primarily IP and growth-led approach.

Crucially, at the same time this discussion was taking place, one specific opportunity had been identified by a group of senior colleagues within the technology team. This related to a fintech called Thought Machine, which was developing a cloud-native next generation banking platform. This provided an ideal pathfinder project and helped to illustrate the broader opportunity within the group.

Solution

'We invest in fintechs who have the potential to really help deliver improvements to the business and service to customers. The more core these solutions sit in our architecture and customer service proposition, the more we consider taking equity stakes.'

Zak Mian, Group Transformation Director

A working group was formed between the central innovation and corporate development teams in order to design solutions for the identified gaps across the end-to-end partnering journey: from idea to execution. The team began by developing a framework for enhancing fintech partnering along key stages of the process.

Their initial steps were to create a shared definition of the key stages in the partnering process. Whilst they identified differing numbers of steps in use across industries, the overall process was similar. They opted for a five-stage process, leveraging definitions already in use in one area of the bank. All those definitions relate to partnering opportunities for a specified business need:

- **Identify.** A long list of relevant fintechs has been identified.
- **Assess.** A selection has been made for a preferred potential partner (typically an initial desktop exercise to form a shortlist and then more detailed interaction with the remaining parties).
- **Engage.** Initial experimentation with the potential partner to test the target partnership solution is being developed or is underway.
- **Advance.** Deployment of the partnership is planned at scale, including a final partnership structure.

Breaking down these processes into these stages enabled them both to build up a cross-group pipeline view and would provide a way to structure potential solutions to the gaps they had identified.

As with many innovation processes, they understood that for each successful partnership reaching the advance stages, many more would need to have been explored and ruled out earlier in the process. Therefore, it was critical that they sourced adequate opportunities from across the bank.

The first step would be to create business-sponsored innovation working groups for their main transformation lines: Retail, Insurance, Commercial and Enterprise (RICE). Each working group would consist of product-level representation, typically from business development, strategy or innovation roles. The working group would become a route through which to disseminate best-practice in terms of fintech scanning, selection and partnering. In addition, additional tooling would be made available to the groups to enable them to execute these activities. For example, access to a central fintech hub was distributed as a way to identify and monitor relevant fintechs across the group, while also providing divisional and group-level data to support decision-making. The working group approach would also provide a way to identify gaps in activity relative to a designated baseline.

Another part of the solution would be to develop a collective understanding of the characteristics of a robust innovation partnership. This would centre on being able to prioritise business needs for which a fintech partner solution had the potential to add the most value relative to a build solution. This would begin by leveraging their initial analysis, but would quickly become enhanced by evidence and experience. At the same time, before selection opportunities to prioritise, they would also need to consider the expected complexity of pursuing them. The netting out of these two characteristics would help to determine which opportunities would be prioritised.

Importantly, they recognised that the complexity of partnering was not a fixed thing. Rather it was something they could aim to improve over time and thereby potentially increase their opportunity space. As such, they would continue to investigate technological and non-technological opportunities to make partnerships easier to deliver, whilst still achieving appropriate levels of safety and security.

At the advance end of the process, they would utilise their pathfinder opportunity alongside non-fintech partnership experience to inform their approach to partnership structuring. A key element of this was consideration of equity investments. Where there was an opportunity to invest, they decided on two core principles that would need to be met. Firstly, they would only consider investing in companies with whom they expected to form a commercial agreement or had done so already. Secondly, there would need to be a very clearly defined strategic benefit of taking equity, relative to what was achievable through a commercial contract. Their initial appetite was also focused on minority investment stakes only, due to the additional consolidation considerations typically associated with larger positions. It was at this point in the process that they would utilise their pathfinder opportunity to begin building some of the specific capabilities required for fintech investing.

In order to oversee the implementation of all these steps and to provide additional senior stakeholder sponsorship, they would create a Corporate Venture Panel (CVP). These sponsors included a senior colleague from each of the RICE areas, along with senior colleagues from enabling areas such as Group Legal and the Chief Technology Office. The panel would initially meet on a quarterly basis to oversee the pan-Group activity, review partnering decisioning and consider investment rationale.

Delivery

'We are not an asset manager, not here to choose the next Klarna, we invest in partners that can help transform our business. When you have an equity stake sponsored by a business unit, rather than a separate investment vehicle, the synergies become more entrenched.'

Carla Antunes da Silva, Group Strategy Director

The mobilisation of the innovation working groups provided a more accurate view of the existing activity levels in each part of the organisation. They found that each area had different strengths and gaps relative to the planned baseline. For example, in some areas they were conducting a lot of market scanning but they were struggling to get momentum behind proper engagements; other areas had excellent momentum behind a limited number of high-profile opportunities, but without the depth of opportunity to ensure sustainable delivery. A tailored development plan was therefore put in place for each area and the central team's support focus was also phased.

Notably, in some areas, the initial market assessments raised more fundamental questions about their innovation priorities. It also took some time to embed the target partner decision framework into the bottom-up work to ensure that the highest potential opportunities were being surfaced. There was also a broader task around building awareness of the partnering opportunity across relevant product and transformation teams. As such, while the opportunity engine had been switching on, there was some lag before it started to generate the desired level of pipeline activity.

The second thing that became apparent is that the friction involved in partner engagement and experiments was creating a bottleneck in the pipeline. Whilst some drop-off was expected between the identify/assess and engage stage, the actual conversion level was below expectations. Qualitative feedback from colleagues also highlighted the time and complexity involved in delivering at this stage. It was also recognised that excessive friction at this point in the process also has the potential to negatively impact the experience for the fintech, for example, by adding additional cost to their side of the partnering activity. The central fintech team has taken ownership of driving forward improvements in this journey by working with relevant process owners to right-size or simplify processes. In addition, they believe that the group's existing technology transformation journey will support a growing number of partnerships over the next one to two years, for example, by improving the availability of APIs to support integration.

Nonetheless, they were able to leverage the early successes to maintain momentum and visibility. For example, case studies and articles were written up and shared with all colleagues via the group's main interchange site. Similarly, the senior sponsorship from the CVP helped to maintain the focus and drive.

As they built up their experience and pooled the learnings across the group, they were able to sharpen their priority spaces and their supporting frameworks. For example, they saw two clusters begin to show the most potential. The first of these was centred on partnering to accelerate or enhance their capabilities in strategically important emerging technologies. The second cluster centred on partnerships that would allow them to extend their customer offering into relevant adjacencies where partnering provided an advantage to developing the adjacent capabilities internally, for example, due to economies of scale or required speed-to-market.

Crucially, their early pathfinder opportunities allowed them to socialise at Executive and Board level as well as via their Corporate Venture Panel. This enabled them to begin to hone their approach to partnership structuring. They had already established that they only planned to make investments where they were confident of a long-term partnering relationship with the fintech. Their intention was then to understand the incremental benefit of pairing the commercial partnering relationship with strategic equity investment.

One of their pathfinder projects in this space was their relationship with Thought Machine.

Since 2017, Lloyds had been completing extensive testing and proofs of concept with Thought Machine's Vault capability, a cloud-native next generation banking platform. They anticipated that the new technology could enable Lloyds to provide customers with more tailored products, as well as enable faster development cycles and further digital banking improvements. In this scenario they found that there were sufficient benefits in making a strategic investment in Thought Machine above and beyond their contractual agreement. For example:

- **Accelerating outcomes.** It would help to fund the development of the core product, enabling swifter product delivery into Lloyds.
- **Demonstrating organisational commitment.** It would signal an enhanced level of organisation commitment to the partnership, supporting deeper collaboration.
- **Financial upside.** Whilst not the primary driver, they believed that Thought Machine was well aligned to future industry technology trends and that their partnership would support the company's growth. The investment allowed them to participate in this future valuation upside.

As a result, the Group's Corporate Development team began to engage on a potential equity investment. In recent years, the team has conducted a number of sizeable acquisitions or disposals of large loan portfolios. Therefore, the consideration of this opportunity provided a very new set of challenges. The team had to adapt in terms of:

- **Valuation method.** Future revenue growth was a much more significant component on the valuation model versus the typical balance sheet approach.
- **Due diligence.** Technical due diligence and IP are significant parts of the process relative to the traditional credit review.
- **Risk analysis.** They had to identify and accept a different blend of risks given the relative age of the company and the stage of product development.

Working closely with the team at Thought Machine, the team adapted to this new type of transaction and Lloyds invested £11 million for a c.10% stake in 2018 as part of the company's Series A round.

Results

The RICE innovation working groups are now all mobilised and are generating a more robust pipeline of opportunities. Since late 2018, when the new structured approach to fintech partnering was introduced, the Group has identified c.2,000 fintechs against 130 specified business needs. A further c.50 opportunities are currently in the engage phase.

Over the course of eight quarterly CVPs, 70 material opportunities have been presented. This has resulted in nine live partnerships and three equity investments. In addition to those that have been supported via CVP, four others have been originated.

Their ability to measure this aggregate pipeline including the performance by stage is itself the result of the successful deployment of their fintech tooling. Moreover, their ability to highlight the challenges of third-party experimentation both quantitatively and qualitatively has increased the collective will to make improvements to their journey.

Perhaps most promisingly, the two thematic opportunity clusters that have emerged have begun to influence strategic planning. They began the activity aiming to respond to the strategic demands of the business areas but now that there is greater visibility of the opportunities that can be opened up through investing, some areas are re-calibrating. For example, they are considering the way they implement and maintain technologies or what business models they might pursue in the future.

Learnings

'Even when you're in "recovery mode" as business, you still have to think about innovation. The problem is that we react faster to threats than we do to opportunities.'

Juan Gomez Reino, Group Chief Technology Officer

Key to the success that the approach is now delivering is having the general principles of when and why they should partner at the heart of the process. By ensuring that all colleagues have a strong understanding of this rationale, they have been able to focus their efforts on higher potential spaces at an earlier stage of the pipeline. Coupling this clear purpose with pathfinder projects helps to translate the intention into action. More specifically, these projects will typically need to have a lot of executive sponsorship in order to carve out new organisational pathways that, once formed, will allow others to follow under more typical levels of sponsorship.

They divided their pipeline into four key stages based on the underlying activity required to take an opportunity from idea through to execution. This staged profile allowed them to create more targeted actions and to identify the ratio of opportunities moving from one stage to another. However, what they also came to realise is that the overall pipeline was only ever as efficient as the weakest link. They needed to spread and synchronise their improvement efforts across the pipeline. Perhaps most notably, having a robust early pipeline connected to a less mature execution capability can lead to disengagement and frustration. Developing the pipeline stages in-sync helps to maintain balanced progress.

Organisations often develop dominant approaches to innovation and change delivery. Much like creating any new habit, their shift to partnering has required a shift in mindset, culture and capabilities. As well as being very clear on the strategic rationale for the change, they have also used a rolling agenda of communications to continue to reinforce the objectives and progress. These communications have targeted different audiences: from all colleagues through to more senior decision-makers. Having the CVP representatives available to support the visibility and mandate of the fintech partnering agenda has also been crucial to driving the required change.

What's Next

Whilst they have enhanced their partnering capabilities over the past two years, there is still a lot more that they need to do to get close to their target state.

As described, the largest constraint on their pipeline remains at the 'engage' stage. Their in-flight technology plans are expected to support greater partnering activity by reducing the cost and complexity of integration. However, they need to do more still on the non-technical side of third party engagements, especially to keep pace with the changing technology capabilities. They will approach this utilising systems thinking to articulate the journey and then working with stakeholders and policy-owners to simplify or right-size where relevant.

Furthermore, they will continue to assess their broader approach retrospectively. Whilst they now have several live partnerships and investments and they believe they have executed them in the right way, they will ultimately measure their success based on their customer and organisational benefits.

Chapter 2
BBVA
Invest through a corporate venture fund

Case: Propel Ventures

Executive Summary

In February 2016, the new $250 million US fund Propel was offi-
cially launched as a fintech venture capital firm. The fund replaced
BBVA Ventures, which was originally founded in 2012 to provide
funding and expertise to promising technology companies disrupting the financial services industry. In establishing Propel as
an independent entity, BBVA did something no other financial
services company had done prior to this. BBVA considered that was
its best option was to be seen as attractive as other non-corporate
investors for the startups that BBVA was interested in supporting.
Being an independent fund gave Propel agility to make decisions
faster and more effectively, which brought more and higher quality
investments to the Group.

With this new structure, Propel was able to compete with the many established venture funds in Silicon Valley. Propel's focus is on early-stage investment opportunities at the intersection of technology and finance. Since its formation, Propel's financial performance has outperformed its own expectations; four of its companies, between the Propel portfolio and BBVA Ventures legacy portfolio, have achieved unicorn status, including two IPO and three exits. Having a team on the ground in the centre of the US startup ecosystem has proved to be essential for BBVA.

Looking forward, the expectation for Propel is that it continues to invest in fintech businesses that provide strategic value and financial returns for BBVA. Thanks in large part to Propel, BBVA has a better insight into the talent and capital that can help it build projects to continue transforming itself.

Introductions

Do you want more details about this case? Find additional highlights from these interviews at www.howbanksinnovate.com.

Javier Rodríguez Soler, CEO, BBVA USA

Javier Rodríguez Soler was named President and CEO of BBVA USA and US country manager for the BBVA Group in January 2019. Most recently he has been overseeing the acquisition of BBVA USA by PNC. He was previously BBVA Group's global head of Strategy and M&A, and before that he was managing director for Corporate and

Investment Banking. Prior to BBVA, Rodríguez Soler was director of Investor Relations and director of Strategy and M&A at Endesa. He was also an engagement manager with McKinsey and Company.

Jay Reinemann, General Partner, Propel Venture Partners

As a partner at Propel, Jay has led investments in Coinbase, Neon and DocuSign, among others. Before BBVA spun off the fund and became a limited partner, Jay led BBVA Ventures including the bank's acquisition of Simple. Prior to Propel, Jay held several positions at Visa in digital transformation, emerging projects, and ecommerce. As head of the Visa Corporate Ventures and Strategic Alliances Group he led investments in information security, mobile and payments technology companies.

Ricardo Forcano, former CIO

Ricardo Forcano was with BBVA from 2011 until 2020, when he decided to leave the bank to start an academic research project. His last role in BBVA was Chief Information Officer and Global

Head of Engineering and Organisation. Ricardo was a member of BBVA Group's Executive Committee and his responsibilities included the bank's technological architecture, the development of next-generation systems and software, the operation of the infrastructure and security. Before that Ricardo was Head of Talent and Cultures and director of Business Development for Growth Markets. As Director of Corporate Strategy, he was responsible for the launch of Propel. Ricardo graduated from the Universidad de Zaragoza in 1995 (MA in Engineering) and has an MSc in Technology and Policy from Massachusetts Institute of Technology.

Background

Key Figures

Total assets: €730 billion
Number of customers: 80 million
Number of branches: 7,500
Number of full-time employees: 120,000
(Approximate as of 2020)

BBVA was founded in 1857 and is today one of the largest financial institutions in Spain. In addition, it is the largest financial institution in Mexico and it also has a significant operation in South America and the US. It also owns 49.85% of Turkey's Garanti BBVA.

BBVA's purpose is to bring the age of opportunities to everyone, with six strategic priorities: improving its clients' financial health, helping its clients transition toward a sustainable future, reaching more clients, driving operational excellence, having the best and most engaged team and having a focus on data and technology. Their overarching value is that the customer comes first, 'we think big and we are one team'. Its responsible banking model aspires to achieve a more inclusive and sustainable society.

The BBVA Group has developed new people management models and new ways of working, which have enabled the bank to keep transforming its operational model, but have also promoted cultural transformation and have favoured the ability to become a purpose-driven company, or, in other words, a company where staff guide their actions according to the company values and are genuinely inspired and motivated by the same purpose.

Problem

'It was necessary to stop being a spectator and become a player in the ecosystem.'

Ricardo Forcano, former CIO

In 2009, parallel to the global financial crisis and at a time when the concept of fintech did not even exist, BBVA had a vision that would radically change the course of its strategy: in a few years a structural crisis was going to occur in the traditional banking business model. Predictably, not only would it be necessary to compete with traditional banks, but all kinds of technology companies, from giants like Google to small startups that were going to enter the financial business. In Silicon Valley, some companies were starting to build interesting financial services projects, especially in the world of payments, and BBVA felt the need to be connected with all the innovation that was emerging there. The need went beyond simply thinking about how to compete with these new companies, but was much more structural. How could a bank change the way it works to adapt to the way these companies use technology?

At that time balance sheet investing, CVC (corporate venture capital), e.g. direct investment by large corporations in external startups, already existed in other industries. BBVA began to explore the strategic initiative of setting up a separate venture capital fund to better understand incipient competitors, without losing sight of the fact that the fund also had to function at a financial level in order to be sustainable and to be a relevant player in the startup ecosystem.

In 2011, Ricardo Forcano, in the Madrid offices, and Jay Reinemann, in San Francisco, joined BBVA in order to promote this initiative. One of the first problems they identified was how to best get in touch with the ecosystem and understand how it works. As such, it was decided that it would be best to invest in a couple of funds that were already dedicated to investing in startups and learn from them. Thus BBVA completed its first investments in Silicon Valley in early 2012 with an investment in the seed-capital fund and incubator 500 startups and the fintech fund Ribbit Capital. In all, 500 startups were founded by investor and entrepreneur Dave McClure, who previously worked with companies such as PayPal, Facebook, LinkedIn, Mint and Microsoft, and Ribbit Capital was a new Silicon Valley-based venture firm led by serial entrepreneur Meyer Malka.

After this experience, BBVA decided to start investing directly in startups. BBVA completed investments in companies such as SaveUp, FreeMonee and SumUp. SaveUp was a startup that partnered with financial institutions to apply gaming techniques to encourage savings, debt reduction and financial education. FreeMonee developed a consumer gift network for retailers to offer gifts to their consumers through their banks. SumUp is a global technology company and the leading mobile point-of-sale (mPOS) company in Europe. Thanks to SumUp's technology, small merchants around the world can accept card payments anywhere using a mobile device.

During these operations, BBVA realized that there was another problem. Due to its corporate and legal implications, the bank's decision-making process was very complex. There were too many layers of decision-making processes, which took too long when agility was necessary to be competitive in the ecosystem. That was when BBVA Ventures, the first specific vehicle in the United States, began to take shape. It was set up in Silicon Valley so it could invest in startups at a much faster pace and this led to the creation of Propel.

BBVA Ventures was originally founded in 2012 to provide funding and expertise to promising technology companies disrupting the financial services industry. Until 2016, the group worked with entrepreneurs and co-investors in the US, Mexico and Europe, becoming a long-term partner in their success. However, captive bank funds have less freedom, less speed, and not a very good perception from early-stage companies.

BBVA was seeing some adverse response to BBVA Ventures, based on the stereotype that some venture capitalists hold against corporate investors. Because they are often gatekeepers to opportunities, BBVA did not always have access to information until potential opportunities were already gone. Startups were wary of corporate venture funds, concerned about conflicts of interest and long-term commitment.

In addition, the US Bank Holding Company Act limits the manner in which banks can invest, stating in some instances that banks can hold no more than five percent of certain ventures. For an early-stage company, that may not amount to much at all, so the bank was sometimes limited to later-stage companies or forced to remove voting rights and the like to remain in compliance with bank regulations. The net effect of being able to invest smaller amounts limited BBVA Ventures role as investor to be more of a follower than a lead investor.

This friction was avoided by the establishment of Propel as an SBIC (Small Business Investment Company).

Solution

If BBVA wanted to become an investor with credibility and prestige with access to the top companies, they came to the conclusion it was necessary to do so from a different position than as a balance sheet investor. BBVA made the decision to establish Propel as an independent entity to replace BBVA Ventures for two key reasons. The first reason was directly tied to the mindset of some startups regarding working with corporate venture funds. BBVA came to understand that some startups believed that they could get better support from the traditional venture capital structure than working with a large banking entity. The traditional venture capital model aligns interests with the startup founders given that the General

Partners managing the fund put personal capital at risk but also benefit from the success of the investment performance. This financial alignment is typically missing in a corporate venture capital program as it would be unusual to ask an employee to contribute their personal funds to their work projects.

Secondly, BBVA Ventures had been structured in the highly regulated US banking market so that it was limited to investing only up to five percent in any given financing round, which limited the range of possible investment opportunities.

The new US fund was a Small Business Investment Company (SBIC), an arrangement to help channel investment dollars to US small businesses. Operating as an SBIC gave BBVA flexibility in stake size, which the bank did not have as a bank-regulated corporate fund. BBVA became a limited partner, contributing all capital to the fund and accepting delegated management of it. It was a rather unique model, as few corporate venture programs had ever taken that step before.

In an increasingly competitive fintech venture capital environment, BBVA believed that its increased capital, combined with the traditional venture capital model of Propel, would enable access to invest in the best fintech startups and better support BBVA's vision of using technology to change financial services for the benefit of the customer.

The shift to Propel as an independent entity made it a more attractive investor for the companies BBVA was interested in supporting and also generated more strategic value from this fund.

Losing control of approved investments posed a risk to the bank. The new entity would have substantial autonomy, and it took a lot of trust and alignment in the legal structure and governance to make it possible.

Two important conditions were established as control measures for Propel:

- The investment scope was made clear in that the kind of companies in which Propel was going to invest in were companies that were strategically interesting for BBVA, such as those at the intersection of finance and technology. Based on those investment perimeters, Propel was able to freely construct a portfolio of investments and manage the business as any other venture fund.

- A quarterly Limited Partner Advisory Council was established to review what investments had been made in the last three months, how the portfolio was doing, updates on the fintech market in general, and other strategic insights brought from the Propel team.

Delivery

'Whilst BBVA prefer to invest through Propel, BBVA still retain the option to invest from its balance sheet, e.g. if it is a very large strategic opportunity where they want to take a much bigger ownership stake or doesn't fit the profile of Propel e.g. post Series A.'

Jay Reinemann, General Partner, Propel

In February 2016, Propel was officially launched as a fintech Venture Capital firm with a Small Business Investment Company license. The news was announced by BBVA, which indicated that it had increased its fintech fund to $250 million from $100 million and partnered with Propel Venture Partners to manage the investment independently from its offices in San Francisco. This capital would be invested in two funds, one in the US and the other globally to make investments mainly in Europe and Latin America.

In order to manage this fund, a small team led by Jay Reinemann was spun out of BBVA in San Francisco. The founding team combined executives from BBVA as well as from the startup ecosystem and venture capital and investment banking fields. It was important to have a team that understood the interests of BBVA, had strong fintech knowledge and networks and could build a successful venture fund business.

The team was given authority to form the business to be competitive with the many large established venture fund competitors in

Silicon Valley. This traditional venture structure enables the financial alignment to attract great investors to the Propel team and win investments into successful startups.

Propel's focus is on early stage (seed and series A) investment opportunities at the intersection of technology and finance. Areas of focus included payments, lending, insurance, wealth management, digital banking, personal financial management and new digital channels.

Results

The launch of Propel in 2016 was met with a positive industry reaction, if not slight confusion about the difference between Propel and BBVA Ventures, a venture arm wholly owned by BBVA. Multiple outlets, including Bank Innovation, Business Insider, TechCrunch and others, covered the news.

In just four years since the formation of Propel, financial performance has outperformed expectations, with four portfolio companies between the Propel portfolio and BBVA Ventures legacy portfolio that have achieved unicorn status, including two IPO and three exits. The group's portfolio companies have created over 10,000 fintech jobs. The team's portfolio includes over 30 startups of which, in the majority of cases, Propel is a lead investor and Board member. This has led to larger ownership positions and more meaningful roles to help the founders/startups build their businesses.

Looking forward, the expectation for Propel is that it continues to invest in great fintech businesses that provide strategic value and financial returns for BBVA and help the global financial services industry to move forward. Through these investments, BBVA can continue to support the fintech ecosystem, but also learn more about the role technology can play in people's financial lives and how the bank itself can adapt its operating model to deliver on customer's changing expectations.

In terms of strategy, it has been essential for all BBVA areas to have a team located at the centre of the startup ecosystem. Frequent contact with companies and people of interest has provided the bank with a wealth of input for its digital strategy and collaborations between the business areas and the 'startups'. Propel's creation has also worked for making initial contacts or leveraging certain M&A operations in the digital world carried out directly by BBVA, such as the purchase of Simple in 2014.

Propel has provided BBVA with insights and intelligence on industry trends and external innovation that is relevant to financial services and has had an invaluable contribution helping to drive connections and business opportunities with the Fintech ecosystem. The team played a key role in sourcing new investment opportunities for BBVA. Propel has also helped drive partnership opportunities with startup companies in several countries of the BBVA footprint, such as the US, Spain, Mexico and Colombia. For example, at the end of 2019 BBVA announced a partnership with leading online marketplace lending platform Prosper to offer customers an innovative digital home equity line of credit product.

Four years later, BBVA's 'venture capital' model as a sole investor, managed autonomously by Propel to facilitate and expedite investments in 'fintech' companies, has become a benchmark for other stakeholders interested in investing in the fintech innovation ecosystem.

Learnings

'If I were to do it again, I'd spend more time understanding the venture capital sector, and meeting with partners in venture capital firms across industries. By doing so, we would have better understood the world of fintechs, venture capital and funding, which may have helped us understand how to set up a firm that would be immediately well received in those circles.'

Javier Rodríguez Soler, CEO, BBVA USA

Propel was created from BBVA Ventures to solve for the dual problems of flexibility in the amount of investment and the challenge around being tied to a corporate investment arm, and the perceived lack of independence in that. Of course, hindsight is 20/20 and launching as an SBIC initially would have been the best course of action.

This leads into one of the most surprising elements of venture capital funding, which is that fintechs and venture capital funds run in a tight circle. The setup, as they had with BBVA Ventures, was outside of that circle, given its direct tie to BBVA. As a result, they missed out on some funding opportunities in which they might have otherwise engaged.

Managing partner for Propel, Jay Reinemann, also made it clear that it is not just about funding fintechs. For as brilliant as fintech founders may be, Jay says it is critical that we remember these companies are startups, and as such money is just one thing they need, the other being support and understanding when it comes to running a company. Not only can the partners at Propel provide that, but, as their strategic partner, BBVA is well-situated to be a key element of their success through the resources they can provide.

Another lesson learned from the Propel experience was the evolution from a 'pull' model to a 'push' model for collaborations between the bank and startups. When the fund was started and the investments in the startups had been made, an effort was made to establish connections between the bank's business areas and the new emerging companies, but it was complicated. When it came to moving forward in the collaboration, problems often arose from both the bank and from the startups themselves. In the end, this model was eventually challenged because it was not giving the expected results. The initial objective for the creation of the fund was to have a radar on the latest fintech trends and have access to the knowledge that could be applied to the bank's transformation and strategies. The way of provoking this talent interchange evolved towards a 'push' model. The first step is now to identify BBVA team's specific needs and analyse which of the startups could help and is keen to resolve concrete business challenges and then a possible collaboration is studied. With this new focus, Propel became a very interesting source of knowledge for BBVA business areas.

Finally, the need to keep abreast on new and global ecosystems of interesting startups is also relevant. With Propel, BBVA started out with a strong focus on Silicon Valley, but over time it began to work on investments in other ecosystems around the world that also offered good opportunities.

What's Next

For more than a decade, BBVA has seen itself as a digital pioneer that embraced the digital revolution in the industry and boldly embraced a vision that leveraged technology as the means to a better experience and more control for customers.

As BBVA moves into the next decade, the bank will continue to leverage this type of mindset to grow and deliver on its purpose of creating opportunities for customers, communities and society in order to secure a future that is sustainable, both from an environmental, social and economic standpoint, and focused on helping people improve their financial health.

Propel's next steps are related to completing the funds' maturity. This means completing the initial investment of $250 million to accompany the companies in which it has invested during this time in their next rounds of financing in order to continue studying possible collaborations between startups and the bank. In the future, BBVA will continue to play a role as an investor in the fintech world for the long term and will continue to bet on the Propel team in any scenario.

The bank has invested $50 million in Sinovation Ventures, the Chinese investment fund specializing in artificial intelligence created by expert Kai-Fu Lee in order to gain access to insights in the growing Chinese market of artificial intelligence innovation. On this path, BBVA will keep a radar on where there is talent and capital in order to build projects that can transform the financial industry.

Chapter 3
Metro
Acquisition

Case: RateSetter

Executive Summary

Metro Bank's (MB) new leadership team was determined to enhance the bank's product portfolio and broaden its existing offerings, as well as diversify and increase the bank's revenue streams.

It sought to identify immediate and near-term ways to achieve these objectives. The bank was eager to have a successful consumer lending business on its books and, after confirming how much it would cost to develop this capability in-house, it decided the best way to achieve its aims was to purchase a successful consumer lending business already active in the market.

The bank's leadership team identified RateSetter (RS) as the ideal acquisition target. The bank got to work quickly, engaging its legal and advisory partners to analyse the rationale for a deal and its potential terms. Following extensive due diligence, the transaction was agreed and quickly completed.

MB and RS created a number of joint working groups, work-streams and project management teams in order to deliver all aspects of the integration project. This was overseen by a streamlined senior management structure, consisting of both MB and RS directors. Teams met regularly and collaborated effectively to deal with challenges as and when they arose.

The bank will continue to leverage RS's mix of product, technology, data and talented team with deep unsecured lending expertise, in order to diversify and grow the bank's revenue streams in the years to come.

Introductions

Do you want more details about this case? Find additional highlights from these interviews at www.howbanksinnovate.com.

Daniel Frumkin, Chief Executive Officer

Dan is responsible for leading the bank with a focus on driving long-term growth by delivering great customer service at the right cost. Prior to joining Metro Bank, Dan worked in the US, the UK, Eastern Europe and Bermuda. He has performed business, risk, product and commercial executive level roles throughout his career. Most recently, Dan was Group Chief Operating Officer at Butterfield Bank with responsibility for eight jurisdictions across the globe, covering a range of business and support areas. Dan has an MBA in Finance and Accounting from the Questrom School of Business at Boston University.

David Thomasson, Chief Commercial Officer

David is responsible for planning, implementing, and managing all product, digital and customer analytics-related functions for Metro Bank. This includes the development of new products and services for customers and delivering the bank's commercial plan. Prior to joining Metro Bank, David's professional career in financial services has been both in the UK at Barclays Bank and more recently in Australia at Macquarie Bank. In that time he has operated in leadership roles across product management, digital, payments, change and operations. He has a BA in History with French from Durham University.

Martin Boyle, Chief Transformation Officer

Martin is responsible for developing and delivering Metro Bank's transformation and change agenda. Prior to joining Metro Bank in 2020, Martin was Chief Transformation Officer at Nationwide

Building Society. He is an experienced change and operations leader, and has also held senior roles in Portman Building Society, VISA Europe and Accenture. He holds a Master of Philosophy (MPhil) in Management Studies from Cambridge University.

Background

Key figures

Total assets: £22.6 billion
Number of customers: 2.2 million
Number of branches: 77
Number of FTE: 3,500
(Approximate as of 31 December 2020)

Since launching in 2010 as the UK's first new high street bank in more than a century, MB now has 77 branches (or stores as they call them) nationwide. It offers a full range of banking services for both personal and business (including SME and corporate) customers, with mortgages, loans and credit cards, as well as a selection of current and savings accounts available.

MB explains its growth by being able to integrate physical and digital delivery. Its 'bricks and clicks' offering provides customers with a service that is different to most other banks, as their branches are, for example, open 7 days a week most weeks of the year.

This sits alongside a mobile and online capability that offers the convenience of banking when and where its customers choose. The bank has hundreds of employees working across a number of innovation teams to achieve its objectives. Divisions such as digital, mobile, customer analytics, and deposits and lending deliver intelligent growth in the banking sector.

In addition, 80% of store managers and 75% of assistant store managers have been promoted from within, demonstrating the loyalty of team members and their dedication to the success of MB moving forward. The bank believes that its colleagues will be the driving force that helps it to become the UK's best community bank.

In 2010, MB launched a mission to bring the revolution to UK banking, while RateSetter (RS) set out to connect borrowers with investors in a new and innovative way. What has been at the heart of both organisations for the past decade is an absolute focus on delivering something better for customers with a real challenger mindset. With both organisations celebrating tenth anniversaries in 2020, it was apt to mark the first milestone by joining forces as this case study explains.

Problem

'We had a problem with our revenue mix, we knew we had to get into the unsecured lending space, it is so obvious since we have such a large current account deposit base.'

David Thomasson, Chief Commercial Officer

2019 was the most challenging year that MB faced since it was launched in 2010. This included making a material adjustment to its Risk Weighted Assets (RWA), periods of net deposit outflows and a delayed senior MREL issuance. These major challenges, together with continued competitive pressures in the residential mortgage market, resulted in a difficult year. Whilst these events materially impacted 2019 financial performance and the share price, the bank retained a simple and resilient balance sheet with a strong capital and liquidity position, providing a solid foundation from which to rebuild.

In February 2020, under fresh leadership, the bank set out a new strategic direction. Enhancing the product portfolio and broadening existing offerings were central to this strategy. Within that, there was a significant drive to diversify and increase the bank's returns over a period of several years.

The bank's management team, led by new CEO Daniel Frumkin, identified unsecured personal lending as a top priority strategic initiative. Building an unsecured personal lending capability had been on the bank's radar for some time, but it now became a key focus to grow revenue and optimise the bank's balance sheet, two pillars of MB's strategy.

There were broadly two paths open to achieve this objective. One was to develop an unsecured lending platform in-house, from scratch. The other option was to purchase an established business, with a strong technology platform and a talented team, offering years of deep experience in the consumer unsecured lending market.

Having a competitive unsecured personal lending offering in place quickly, to play a key role in boosting the bank's returns, was considered a crucial motivating factor. It was decided that the most effective way to streamline this process would be to purchase an existing, successful consumer lending business. The bank began a market-wide scan of potential targets.

After careful consideration and investigation from Metro Bank's board and senior executives, the bank identified RateSetter as the ideal acquisition target.

RS was founded in 2010, just as MB was. It is the UK's most popular peer-to-peer lender with over 750,000 people having invested or borrowed through the platform. Since inception, the business has originated more than £4 billion of lending.

The bank got to work quickly, engaging partners including Jeffries and McKinsey to analyse the rationale for a deal and its potential terms. Legal advisors were also engaged at an early stage. The bank's senior directors engaged in conversations and meetings with counterparts at RS and following negotiation entered a period of exclusivity.

After a period of extensive due diligence and board approval, the transaction was announced, subject to shareholder and regulatory approval. Approval was received and the transaction completed in September.

The bank's existing cash resources were sufficient to fund the purchase of RS. It was agreed that RS's stake in RateSetter Australia (now Plenti Group) would not be included in the transaction and would be retained by RS shareholders.

Since this transaction took place during the Covid pandemic, the transaction was all completed without any face-to-face meetings, with stakeholders working from home and all business conducted via video calls.

Solution

'At its core retail banking, and the products we offer, have been around for a very long time and as such the innovation needs to happen in how you deliver it, making it easier and quicker for the customer.'

Daniel Frumkin, Chief Executive Officer

The case for the bank to purchase RS, as opposed to another unsecured personal lending provider or building an in-house solution, was compelling. RS and MB share a focus on delivering something better for the customer. The pairing of MB's strong deposit base and desire to put these deposits to work with RS's track record of originating and managing credit made strong strategic logic.

RS's originating and underwriting capability will enable the bank to rapidly accelerate its unsecured lending ambitions via an existing, scalable platform. The acquisition also presented an attractive opportunity for MB to improve its lending yield.

With RS, MB anticipates originating significant volumes of loans in 2021. The alternative, building the capability organically, would not see the bank originating meaningful consumer lending volumes until early 2023, and would cost considerably more to build from scratch. The directors at MB are also confident of high near-term profitability, aiming to nearly break even in the first year after purchase before generating significant annual profits by year three.

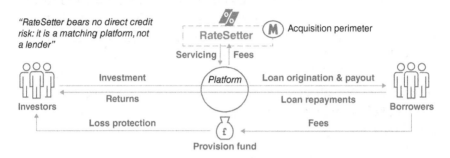

Another attractive consideration for MB was that the acquisition of RS offered a range of hard-to-replicate ancillary benefits. RS's experienced leadership team complemented the bank's own and it has a mature consumer credit capability. Their track-record in growing new business lines and in maturing a technology-led business were considered especially useful.

RS's technology operating model was deemed advantageous, with its delivery hub having the potential to provide a valuable pattern for efficiently scaling MB's delivery capability.

RS's financials demonstrated a scalable consumer credit capability, with credit scorecards and decisioning refined over almost 10 years. RS showed a consistent and reliable credit performance.

The bank estimated that it would cost upwards of £20 million and take many years to build and scale-up an equivalent technology platform.

Therefore, the acquisition of RS was compelling value for money: an initial £2.5 million, with up to an additional £0.5 million payable 12 months after completion subject to the satisfaction of certain criteria and up to £9 million payable on the third anniversary of the completion of the transaction, subject to the satisfaction of certain key performance criteria.

MB did not acquire the backbook of RS loans, which continues to be managed by RS.

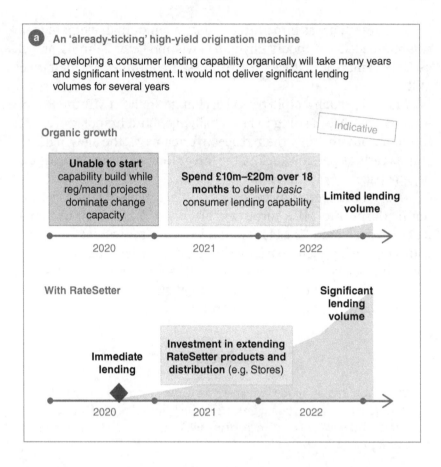

a An 'already-ticking' high-yield origination machine

Developing a consumer lending capability organically will take many years and significant investment. It would not deliver significant lending volumes for several years

Organic growth

Indicative

Unable to start capability build while reg/mand projects dominate change capacity

Spend £10m–£20m over 18 months to deliver *basic* consumer lending capability

Limited lending volume

2020   2021   2022

With RateSetter

Significant lending volume

Immediate lending

Investment in extending RateSetter products and distribution (e.g. Stores)

2020   2021   2022

Keeping the existing talent and expertise within RS's operations, and fusing that with the MB team was considered of the utmost importance. It was clear that all RS colleagues possessed knowledge and experience in unsecured lending that was simply not well developed within MB.

Much like MB, RS was known for its customer focus and strong entrepreneurial and challenger mindset, which makes the two organisations a great cultural fit, with the collective experience and skillset creating a powerful combination to deliver for both MB and RS customers and colleagues alike.

As a result, it was imperative that RS's senior management team was retained. Co-founders Rhydian Lewis and Peter Behrens, as well as Chief Financial Officer Harry Russell continued in their roles at RS.

Managing such a rapid period of change, for both MB and RS colleagues was always going to be a challenge. Both brands were keen to secure buy-in from their respective teams to the new partnership as early as possible, before the integration of the two businesses began apace.

Despite the overall success of the initial integration of RS's lending platform into MB's infrastructure, there were of course challenges to overcome. The bank initially wanted individual functional teams to develop their respective integration designs, but shifted the approach to have a top-down steer on all designs and principles. The lesson was learned early on that a target state needs to be defined from top-down, rather than bottom-up.

Delivery

'It was a marriage made in heaven, they had operational capability to scale quickly, they had a great tech stack, well designed and validated, and they had credit expertise – which we didn't. What we had was liquidity.'

Martin Boyle, Chief Transformation Officer

In order to begin delivering results with immediate effect, MB created a dedicated integration programme that was sponsored by the bank's Chief Transformation Officer, Martin Boyle.

The programme was overseen by a streamlined senior management team, which centrally managed all activity. The MB directors involved in the project gave a significant amount of their time to overseeing the programme each week, considering its status as a key strategic objective.

In order to allocate resources effectively, a series of work-streams were set up to focus on specific areas. Chief among these were:

- Growing the business
- People
- Analysing and managing risk
- Ensuring IT functionality
- Central functions
- Legal considerations

Each work-stream had joint business owners, one from MB, one from RS, with a project manager and a sponsor from MB's Executive Committee.

A comprehensive communications framework was instigated to keep the project moving forward. Kick-off workshops were provided for people from both MB and RS that were involved in the integration programme, along with subsequent follow-ups to address any concerns amongst colleagues. Daniel Frumkin and Rhydian Lewis, the respective CEOs of MB and RS, attended these meetings to emphasise their importance and be on-hand to answer questions from across the two organisations.

These were supplemented by town hall style events, primarily for RateSetter colleagues, to introduce them to the MB brand and culture and what to expect from the integration plans. A range of communications were issued to colleagues from both sides as key milestones were achieved, for example when joint lending was activated post-acquisition.

Ensuring that the integration did not overshoot its budget whilst sticking to pre-agreed delivery timescales was a recurrent challenge for the bank. Its senior directors initiated a steering committee to oversee holistic progress of the project, meeting every fortnight but shifting to a monthly format once they were confident that a reliable delivery rhythm was in progress.

Each work-stream met weekly in their own working groups to develop and manage plans, assess risks and overcome pressing issues. It was quickly discovered that some work-streams occasionally felt they were operating in isolation, and ensuring a high level of understanding across the separate work-streams was a constant challenge. A weekly programme board meeting had been brought together across all work-stream teams from the outset, which helped to tackle this problem. This also aided in overseeing day-to-day delivery and cross-programme activity. On occasion, ad-hoc working groups were also established to focus on specific topics that required immediate attention.

Combined together, these various work-streams, steering committees and working groups reported centrally to senior MB and RS colleagues. This kept both organisations united and well-informed of progress against objectives. Teams from across both organisations reported back that having senior level sponsorship for each work-stream and the programme overall meant there was a high level of accountability and constant motivation to hit targets. Having a dedicated "grow the business" work-stream was also considered useful, as it encouraged collaborative thinking early on and helped colleagues from both sides to begin envisioning themselves as a cohesive unit moving forward.

Results

As key milestones were ticked off, the integration of the two businesses matured and results started to become apparent. MB's acquisition of RS completed in September 2020, with MB-funded lending via RS commencing just a few weeks later in October 2020. MB and RS's digital channels became more intricately linked towards the end of the year, opening up MB branded channels using RS's functionality in early 2021.

The bank is applying common sense when integrating functions from across the two businesses, doing this in a phased approach. Simple, easy-to-implement changes were made quickly, and more complicated functions went through a more robust design and implementation process.

The initial lending launch was considered a success, arriving soon after the completion of the acquisition and with no major technical or operational issues being reported. Whilst it is too early to report on achievement of commercial targets, initial results are encouraging. There may also be opportunities to utilise RS's brand and capabilities elsewhere, to explore other lines of revenue generation such as motor finance.

The bank is positive that it will be able to leverage the combined strengths of MB and RS to continue growing the unsecured lending book, achieving its core objective of greater diversification and growth in its revenue streams. The value of its loan originations in the coming months and years will be the most crucial KPI as a key pillar of the bank's strategy going forward.

Learnings

Having a strong commercial focus was crucial to staying on track with delivering the project. Never losing sight of the original objective, to help diversify and grow the bank's revenue streams, gave everyone involved an overarching focus point.

As mentioned, MB originally wanted to enable the various functional teams to develop their own individual integration designs. However, it quickly learnt that this was an inefficient approach that hampered productivity and reduced consistency across the project. The bank shifted the approach to have a top-down steer on designs and principles.

With hindsight, MB would also have used its cross work-stream approach more prominently when it came to release management of the different integration functionalities. The main reason was that it would have been a great help in overcoming some of the silo issues that cropped up in a few specific working groups.

What's Next

With regards to the ongoing integration the bank will implement a multibrand strategy in order to leverage both businesses' strengths.

Five key integration principles have been identified, which are:

- **Prioritise growth.** Lending is to be ramped up gradually in early 2021, initially via RS's own channels before RateSetter becomes the lending engine for MB branded loans available for customers both in-store and online.
- **Develop a compelling offer.** Provide a seamless digital user experience with instant pricing to drive conversions and customer retention, calibrate pricing to increasingly attract low interest rate risk segments and implement enhanced RS Quote API solutions.
- **Retain key talent.** Build a supportive, exciting and engaging work culture attracting leading digital talent and preventing attrition.
- **Integrate business areas.** Provide whilst not diminishing key capabilities required for growth.
- **Leverage RateSetter capabilities to transform MB.** Include nearshore and offshore centres, channelling RS's entrepreneurial mind-set as part of MB's ongoing transformation.

There is a clear path for innovating together in the next decade, growing revenue streams in the process. The RateSetter brand will be used for aggregator and direct channels, with the expectation that significantly more volume can be achieved on price comparison websites, which are predicted to become increasingly important across the unsecured lending space in the future.

Away from its relationship with RateSetter, MB launched into the specialist mortgages market in late 2020, transforming its products and criteria. The bank has plans to innovate further in this space, stating its ambition to become the UK's number one specialist lender. This forms a key part of MB's revised strategy, as it seeks a better yielding asset book and improved returns by rebalancing its lending mix towards areas such as niche mortgages, SME banking and unsecured loans.

It also continues to play an active role in overhauling technology in the business banking landscape, with new products and services as part of its commitment to the Capability and Innovation Fund.

Chapter 4
J.P. Morgan Acquisition

Case: InstaMed

J.P.Morgan

Executive Summary

J.P. Morgan (JPM) wanted to better serve its clients by expanding its footprint in the healthcare industry, with the ultimate goal of disrupting the broken status quo of healthcare payments. The bank explored options to build a new platform and solutions-based business from scratch, while also scanning the market for potential partners and acquisition opportunities.

Healthcare is complex and fragmented, which is compounded further by the rapid growth of the market over the last two decades without showing signs of slowing down. Despite the projected growth, the industry has been slow to modernise its payments processes, causing pain points across the spectrum of users.

In July 2019, the bank acquired InstaMed (IM) as a wholly owned subsidiary. The acquisition of IM allowed the bank to differentiate itself in three distinct areas in the healthcare payments space: the power of a healthcare payments network, innovation in a legacy environment, and ensuring high standards in security and compliance. IM helps solve pain points felt by all stakeholders: providers, payers and consumers.

The fintech offered the bank the ability to quickly leapfrog into the healthcare payments market. The acquisition of the fintech will give the bank an advantage in one of the fastest growing sectors. In the future, both the bank and IM plan to increase the reach of the combined strengths and capabilities to more of the industry.

Introductions

Do you want more details about this case? Review all the highlights from the in-depth interviews at www.howbanksinnovate.com.

Martha Beard, Managing Director, Head of North America Receivables, J.P Morgan Wholesale Payments

Before her current role, Martha was the North America Head of JPM's Treasury Services Corporate Sales franchise within the

Corporate and Investment Bank. She previously oversaw the Wholesale Payments Healthcare business including the integration of IM. During her nearly 30-year career with JPM, she has held a variety of positions. Notably, as Product Executive for Healthcare Solutions, Martha's advocacy with members of Congress for administrative simplification across financial transactions on the Affordable Care Act led to further work with the Congressional Budget Office on scoring of the legislation. Martha is a graduate of Rutgers University's Center for Women's Senior Leadership Program and has a Bachelor of Arts from the University of Kentucky.

Bill Marvin, CEO of InstaMed, Managing Director & Head of Healthcare Payments, J.P. Morgan

Bill co-founded IM in 2004 and since the acquisition Bill continues to lead IM as CEO, and he is also Managing Director & Head of Healthcare Payments at JPM. Prior to IM, Bill was an executive in Accenture's Health and Life Sciences practice, where he worked with senior executives at clients such as UnitedHealth Group and US Prior to Accenture. Bill founded CareWide (now a part of Allscripts after three acquisitions), which developed Microsoft-based software for submitting electronic claims and managing provider offices. Bill graduated from the University of Pennsylvania with a Bachelor of Arts in Economics.

Background

Key figures:

Total assets: $31 trillion
Total deposites: $683 billion (Approximate as on 2020)

J.P. Morgan's Corporate & Investment Bank includes banking, markets and securities services. The bank supports corporations, governments and institutions across 100+ countries. The Corporate & Investment Bank provides strategic advice, raises capital, manages risk and extends liquidity in markets.

Wholesale Payments at J.P. Morgan represents Treasury Services, Merchant Services, Trade and Commercial Card. Wholesale Payments clients make payments anywhere in the world, in any currency, using any method of payment. The Wholesale Payments business processes more than 106 million transactions worth $6 trillion daily, in more than 120 currencies.

Problem

Like most banks JPM supports a number of verticals, one of which is healthcare. There are a number of challenges in the sector, such as the complexity of the end-to-end payments process. The bank saw this as a problem that could be fixed, an opportunity to not only help existing clients, but also lift up the industry as a whole for a better experience for everyone. They have a number of long-standing clients in the healthcare industry, including large health systems and national health plans, who experience these pain points in the form of high administrative costs and lost revenue. Determined to serve these clients better it needed to expand its footprint in the healthcare industry with the ultimate goal of disrupting the broken status quo of healthcare payments.

Healthcare payments are complex and fragmented. These issues are compounded by the growth of the market over the last two decades without showing signs of slowing down. In fact, according to the Centers for Medicare & Medicaid Services, US healthcare spending is expected to reach $6.2 trillion by 2028.

Despite the projected growth, the majority of the healthcare industry has been slow to modernize its payments processes, causing pain-points across the spectrum of users. The CAQH 2019 Index found that industry spends $40.6 billion on complex administrative transactions between providers and payers, which the report also states could be greatly reduced by converting to fully electronic processes.

For consumers, the payment experience in healthcare is usually in complete contrast to the digital and automated payments found in other industries such as retail and hospitality. Instead, consumers often receive mailed paper statements weeks after a provider encounter and must pay with a paper check.

This experience has been exacerbated by the continuing trend of shifting more financial responsibility to consumers through higher deductibles. The Kaiser Family Foundation reports that more than 80% of workers had a deductible in 2020, up 70% from a decade ago, with the average individual deductible at more than $1,650. High deductible health plans require consumers to pay for many provider services until the deductible is met before the health plan will cover the costs.

However, healthcare and payments are two highly regulated, targeted and scrutinized industries, so bringing those two together requires the highest standards in security and compliance. The effort to build a compliant and secure payments network for healthcare that upheld those standards would take considerable time and effort. The bank determined the needs of their clients and the industry as a whole required more immediate actions and decided to look for partners to expedite the process.

The bank found that many fintechs in the healthcare payments space were only competent in one area, such as patient collections or claim payments to providers, but did not offer payment services for the full scope of the industry. Often, fintechs that appeared from afar to cover a broad range of payments in healthcare, actually had bolt-on services with other partners. A recurring example of this in the industry were the payment processors that needed to partner with gateways to meet the full range of payments for their healthcare clients. It was deemed that no time or effort would be saved for the bank by working with fintechs that relied on multiple and disparate systems, in an already broken and fragmented space.

That was the situation until the bank found IM. JPM saw a unique opportunity to acquire an innovative healthcare platform that was operating at scale. With IM, the bank discovered it could offer healthcare providers, payers and consumers an end-to-end healthcare payments solution in a fraction of the time it would take to build a solution from scratch or by working with multiple partners.

Solution

'Ten years ago InstaMed might have lost business to a bank because the bank had a stronger and longer relationship with that client. Today having the right technology has become much more important.'

> Bill Marvin, CEO of InstaMed and Managing Director
> & Head of Healthcare Payments, J.P. Morgan

In July 2019, JPM acquired IM as a wholly owned subsidiary with the goal to disrupt the healthcare payments space. It was ultimately determined that the acquisition of IM, a scaled company with proven solutions, would allow the bank to leapfrog ahead quickly and arm the bank with real product differentiation in healthcare payments, while focusing on other healthcare initiatives to enhance product offerings for clients.

Together with the new acquisition the bank set out to transform the future of healthcare payments without the heavy burden and extensive time of building a new solution or partnering with multiple fintechs. The investment in a complete payment and remittance management solution allowed the bank to demonstrate its commitment to the healthcare industry and its clients with the promise of delivering new, innovative offerings that make the payments experience better.

IM allowed JPM to differentiate itself in three distinct areas, not seen elsewhere in the healthcare payments space, with the power of a healthcare payments network, relentless innovation in a legacy environment and the highest standards in security and compliance.

Historically, stakeholders, processes and transactions in health-care payments have been siloed by disparate systems and are heavily dependent on human intervention to move forward. This, at its core, is the cause of many challenges within the healthcare payments market, especially high costs of administrative processes. The heavy segmentation and disjointed processes were determined to be a major hurdle for JPM to solve for the complexities of the healthcare payments market.

With the IM Network, the bank found the infrastructure it needed to streamline the healthcare payments without taking the time and resources to build its own. IM allows the bank to connect the industry stakeholders in one payments network, built from the ground up and designed for healthcare. Developed in-house, the IM network powers a broad offering that spans healthcare payment transactions and connects over half of provider organisations with millions of consumers and every type of payer. The network also supports integration into any healthcare IT system to deepen the connections between stakeholders further, while streamlining the payments processes.

The ability to build this type of network would have taken the bank a decade or more to complete. Instead, the bank only needed a fraction of the time with the acquisition and now can move money easier to simplify the healthcare payments process.

As healthcare relies on paper and manual processes for pay-ments, innovation seemed relegated to simple offerings already popular in other industries, such as accepting online payments or sending electronic statements. JPM saw a need to push the healthcare industry beyond business as usual so that clients, both current and future, could realise the benefits of payment innovation.

Not only does IM drive adoption of electronic and digital payments in healthcare, the company also continuously develops and looks to the future payment innovation to maintain forward progress. An innovator in digital healthcare transactions, IM has pioneered new concepts and an advanced technology platform to create a better healthcare experience. For example, IM developed and launched Member Payments in 2013, which was the first solution to connect consumers to providers for payments through their health plan portal.

As a regulated entity, the bank puts security and compliance as one of its highest standards to protect and ensure the trust of customers and clients. The move into the healthcare payments space would need to meet the same standards.

Healthcare is a prime target for malicious data attacks. Healthcare organisations transmit highly personal and sensitive information as part of the normal course of business, from eligibility verification between the provider and payer, and all the way to consumer payments to the provider. The value for healthcare data on the black market is high. Data particularly at risk includes social security numbers, birth dates, payment card information and insurance coverage identification.

JPM does not have to slow down or stop its digital payment transformation in healthcare to consider compliance regulations or mitigate the risks of a breach with the acquisition of IM. In IM, the bank found the opportunity to uphold their high values of security and compliance through an HIPAA and PCI compliant platform that is certified at the highest levels for payments and healthcare. IM also meets and exceeds service levels standards for system availability, redundant backup data and disaster recovery.

The acquisition of IM allows the bank to quickly scale its goals of connecting a disjointed payments space, drive innovation over outdated processes, while maintaining the bank's standards of security and compliance.

Delivery

'We established a collaborative approach to expose InstaMed to our wider payments business to jumpstart innovation and share expertise.'

Martha Beard, Managing Director, Head of North America
Receivables, J.P. Morgan Wholesale Payments

After the acquisition the necessary work was done and completed to integrate the payments network and solutions on the bank's payments rails.

The wave of consumer healthcare payment responsibility skyrocketed at the beginning of the twenty-first century with double digit annual growth. Over the last two decades, deductibles have contributed to both the number of consumers who owe more and the increasing amounts of those balances for medical bills. Additionally, the individual insurance marketplace allows more consumers the opportunity to purchase health plan coverage directly. At the same time, consumers are almost completely saturated by and entrenched in the digital world and bring those experiences to their expectations for healthcare payments, where the majority of processes are manual and paper based.

It was important for the bank to connect consumers with their healthcare payments in a way that would give them back a feeling of control. Through the reach of the bank, even more consumers get a modern experience with their healthcare bills, whether it is patients paying medical bills or health plan members paying their monthly premiums. With JPM and IM, consumers get clarity around their healthcare payments and fast, easy means of making and tracking payments.

As payment responsibility increases for medical bills, healthcare providers are left to collect more often from their patients and for higher amounts. However, providers still rely on paper and manual processes for their patient collections. The bank found that if providers were to tap into the power of the digital age, time to payment for patient collections would not only improve, but providers would also greatly improve the overall experience for their patients.

For provider clients, whether a large health system or a small medical practice, the new offering supports them in delivering a better healthcare payment experience for their patients and staff that improves collections through digital and automated tools, while also increasing patient satisfaction. The integration reduces administrative costs by streamlining processes that typically rely on mailed paper statements and human intervention.

Payers have been a cornerstone of the healthcare industry for the last century. However, their way of doing business faces pressure from the entire industry, which is compounded by shifts in federal mandates and competition from leaders in retail. Payers still have the advantage in the industry with their extensive networks and vast amounts of data. To maintain their position, improving the member experience and streamlining payments to providers will be crucial initiatives for payer organisations.

Payers, health insurance plans and third-party administrators can manage all of their healthcare payments through the platform, including B2B payments from the payer to the provider for claim reimbursement, premium payments from members and employer groups and member payments from consumers to providers through a health plan website.

The new proposition now has the opportunity to bring together the entire healthcare industry for payments, including consumers, providers and payers. IM's tech stack on JPM rails delivers electronic transactions, securely moving money and related healthcare data to the benefit of all those involved in the healthcare payment ecosystem. The integration solves for the pain points felt by all three industry stakeholders in equal measure. The focus on all segments of the market through the IM platform allows JPM to truly achieve the goal of streamlining healthcare payments.

Results

The intention to acquire IM by JPM was announced in 2019. Within a year, JPM and IM became the largest healthcare network of combined clients (providers and payers) and consumers to improve flow data and funds. Together, JPM and IM now have payment relationships with:

- 50% of US consumers
- 50% of US providers
- 8/10 of the largest payers

The scale and resources of JPM combined with the relentless innovation of IM now delivers:

- Expanded payment acceptance for clients (non-clinical and pharmacy)
- Faster funding (same and next day) for clients
- Single healthcare platform for clients with integration of Healthcare Link

IM will continue to offer a strong basis for JPM to better serve consumers, providers and payers, while growing its healthcare payments business, with four specific opportunities:

- Integrate payments (Merchant Acquiring and Payout options) to the IM platform, to be sold as a 'bundle', especially to smaller clients.
- Cross-Sell payments and other JPM products to IM's client base (that are also JPM's prospects).
- Offer IM to existing clients, thereby adding value and creating a stronger and more sticky relationship with those clients.
- Augment consumer offering with potential consumer integration for consumer bill pay.

In the future, JPM and IM will increase the reach of the combined strengths and capabilities to more of the industry. Being part of the bank (with the treasury service solutions, lending strength, technology investment commitment, brand and scale) will allow IM to engage a JPM banker to support their client's broader financial and treasury needs. JPM offers more complete revenue cycle solutions to its existing and prospective healthcare client base.

Learnings

'Given the large scope of integration across all of our client channels, I would work closer with all of the individual business units involved to better calibrate their integration playbooks to get to "business as usual" quicker.'

Martha Beard, Managing Director, Head of North America
Receivables, J.P. Morgan Wholesale Payments

The bank always looks at buy, build, partner options and, as part of this, explored the option of building a new platform and solutions-based business from scratch while also scanning the market for potential partners and acquisition opportunities.

By acquiring IM, JPM significantly accelerated the time-to-market compared with the other alternatives that were available. This included building its own network or creating a series of partnerships with other fintech players that only served one segment of the healthcare payments market. Either option would take years for JPM to get up and running at full speed, while the problems in the industry, including for JPM clients, only got worse. In this case, it made the most sense to move forward with an acquisition of a scaled company with proven solutions that serves all industry stakeholders and to leapfrog ahead quickly while focusing on other initiatives to continue to enhance healthcare offerings for customers and clients.

What's Next

The journey to improve payments in healthcare has in many ways just started. In the coming years JPM will continue to leverage IM's industry expertise, experience, and technology and use the scale and resources of the bank to make an even bigger impact.

The bank hopes the acquisition will continue to deliver benefits to clients of both IM and JPM:

- Deliver IM's healthcare payments solution using the scale of JPM and its payments capabilities.
- Create a better experience for providers, payers, and consumers, who are looking for an easier way to pay and get paid.
- Drive electronic healthcare payment transactions and eliminate the friction of paper and manual processes.

Part II
Build

Chapter 5
Crédit Agricole Incubate Ideas

Case: La Fabrique

Executive Summary

Articulating at the same time incremental and breakthough innovation schemes is not easy and Crédit Agricole (CA) searched for the best way to put innovation into motion. A search for more agility and innovation led CA to take a closer look into the startup ecosystem, and try and replicate the best from their approach to tackling problems and explore new business models, new services and market opportunities.

CA felt that a corporate startup studio would preserve the natural advantages of the independent model and layer it with a set of undeniable unfair advantages from the bank for the future startups to be launched, such as expertise and reputation on the financial market, authorisations and certifications, and access to a well-established distribution network, amongst many others.

La Fabrique by CA started by gathering a team of experienced people with a complementary set of skills that allowed quick delivery and results on the first projects. The studio also defined a five-step ideation process and five innovation territories in order to focus the efforts during the ideation phase. Today, the team has reached its full capacity and works on delivering new fintechs to the world, with the support of the Group.

After two years of experimentation and innovation, La Fabrique by CA has launched six startups and is working on two new projects for 2021.

Introductions

Do you want more details about this case? Find additional highlights from these interviews at www.howbanksinnovate.com.

Eric Caen, Chief Digital Officer, Crédit Agricole

In 1985, Eric co-founded Titus Interactive, a videogame editor that he grew from 3 to 1,000 people and made one of the largest video game companies in France, before a successful IPO in 2005.

He then worked across a number of roles in companies in the US, UK and France. Whilst working as the Chief Digital Officer at CMA CGM, a French container transportation and shipping company, his focus was on adopting artificial intelligence, machine learning, and data. He became the Chief Digital Officer of the bank Crédit Agricole in 2020. He also acts as a board member to several institutions such as Interplay Entertainment and the French Chess Federation.

Laurent Darmon, CEO, La Fabrique by Crédit Agricole

Laurent graduated in Finance and holds a PhD in Information Science on Consumer Satisfaction. He started his career at BNP Paribas and then joined CA, first in the General Inspection department and then in several management positions across financing. As of 2011, Laurent moved towards SaaS and fintechs and became CEO of Teotys, a digital publisher specialising in customer management. In 2013, he was involved in the bank's digital transformation and piloted a programme of modernisation of IT production, before taking charge of Digital Transformation. In 2018, Laurent co-founded La Fabrique by CA, the bank's startup studio. Meanwhile, as a business advisor, Laurent supports the development of several startups and SMEs.

Anaïs Desmoulins, COO, La Fabrique by Crédit Agricole

Anaïs graduated from ESSEC in 2012 and spent eight years working in Product Development and Digital Transformation at Capgemini Consulting. After working across a number of different sectors, the last five years she has been focused on financial services. Anaïs was involved in startups acquisitions for larger banks and deploying innovation labs. She co-founded La Fabrique by CA in 2018.

Background

Key Figures

Total assets: €1.8 trillion
Number of customers: 51 million
Number of branches: 11,000
Number of full-time employees: 143,000
(Approximate as of 2020)

Crédit Agricole (CA) was founded in 1885 and is today the largest network of cooperative and mutualist banks in the world. In France, CAg is composed of 39 Regional Banks and is listed through Crédit Agricole SA, an intermediate holding company, on Euronext Paris' first market and is part of the CAC 40 stock market index.

The bank has a long-lasting tradition of proximity and usefulness towards its clients and has been keen on steering human and digital in its digital transformation strategies, to achieve a hybrid model that would make the most of the two worlds, for its clients, but also for its teams. A search for more agility and breakthrough innovation has led CA to take a closer look into the startup ecosystem, and try and replicate the best from their approach to tackling problems. Whilst working with external partners might have seemed to be the fastest way at first, it created other problems, such as the need to develop new processes, managing data and security, which turned out to be not the most cost-effective approach. Even with acquisitions, the true cost and potential synergies are far from certain.

In 2018, in order to stretch its values and ambitions further, CA decided to entrust its corporate startup studio La Fabrique by CA with disruptive innovation and a mission: industrialising a startup creation and fostering the hybridization of the home-made startups with the Group.

Problem

'One of our biggest challenges is to help our team embrace innovation and change. Some think that technology will make their roles redundant, when in reality we only want to use tech to remove the boring tasks. Freeing them up helps customers with more complex, exciting and interesting requests instead.'

Eric Caen, Chief Digital Officer, Crédit Agricole

The rise of fintechs in every line of financial services has shown to be excessively fast and predatory for Net Banking Income. For example, the foreign exchange market has seen the birth and rise of French fintech iBanFirst, simplifying and securing operations in foreign currencies for SMEs. In 2019, CA saw a drop of 20% in its FX operations with SMEs, while iBanFirst declared a 100% increase in benefits. One of many examples of how a customised and simplified user experience makes a powerful difference. Another example is to be found on the professional market, and especially banking services to independent workers. Newcomers such as Qonto, Revolut for Business and Shine, in France, have grown from nothing to owning about 10% of market shares over only two years. Moreover, incumbents also have opened the door to new practices and needs, stretching banking outside of the bank (online, marketplaces, retailers) and multiplying extra-banking sets of offers to partner with their clients better on a long-term basis.

The rise of fintechs is quick and implacable. In order to find the right elements of answers for the bank CA, the first challenge was to list all the innovation initiatives within the bank, bringing together 39 Caisses Régionales (Regional Banks with their own development strategies and territorial sovereignty) and acknowledge the difficulty to realise the bank's digital transformation and lead, at the same time as disruptive thinking about the market, banking services and beyond. That is when a team led by Laurent Darmon and Anaïs Desmoulins was assigned with the task of defining a way to foster disruptive innovation to the benefit of CA and its clients. They started by sharing two convictions that were essential to the birth of the future corporate startup studio:

1. **Incremental changes are no game changers.** Project management as it is traditionally done in corporations aims for incremental changes to existing offers and practices. Very rarely should they result in disruptive changes because they were simply never meant to. In order to get a broader view on market trends and greater ideas to take the lead on the pace of change, it was necessary to take a step aside from the bank and its usual incremental improvements.

2. **Disruption calls for unswerving sponsorship.** It was also very clear that such a step aside from the bank would make it difficult to come back with ideas, ready to be branched onto existing offers and services and work on the hybridisation with the bank. Hence, it would be crucial to ensure a constant and total sponsorship from leaders, in order to transform ideas into a collective success.

With these two convictions in mind, the quest for the best model to follow could begin.

| | Option A
A corporate programme
in an external incubator | Option B
A corporate accelerator | Option C
An intrepreneurship
programme |
|---|---|---|---|
| **Pros** | Externalised functioning costs | Solid/proven products to build from | People working 'close from home', with the knowledge of the Group's culture, processes and ambitions |
| | Cross-business synergies with other companies | Experienced entrepreneurs and teams | |
| **Cons** | External entrepreneurs with ideas that could not all fit with the Group's roadmap | Shared capitalisation with potential competitors, especially on fintech products | Heavy investment in terms of human resources, also difficult to bring back to their initial occupation in case of failure of the startup |
| | The risk of not transforming the startup into business for the Group by being too far away from core activities | Mature products that could be difficult to spin in order to fit with the Group's processes and tech | Lack of diversity in the profiles of entrepreneurs |

Solution

'The studio is the link between the bank's strategy and execution.'

Laurent Darmon, CEO, La Fabrique by Crédit Agricole

First, the team started exploring existing models and solutions and reported back to the bank. The startup ecosystem in Paris has evolved a lot in the past 10 years, especially with the recent opening 'Station F', the largest startup incubator in Europe. Multiple models showed interesting advantages but also critical flaws when projected on to the bank's environment.

CA found through its research that many companies would launch corporate acceleration programmes in partnership with existing and recognised incubators in the 2010s, with the idea of both identifying promising startups to invest in and to co-develop with entrepreneurs new offers and experiences to be tested before a large-scale implementation within the company's markets. Many companies still invest in these mentoring programmes today, as they represent the least engaging way to benefit from the startup ecosystem and associated good press, but also are very easy to shut down in case of a change in priorities. Most of the functioning costs rely on the partner incubator and the teams benefit from the presence of other startups and programmes around to learn from. This transversality, which will prove to be one of the key challenges in startup studios, is also operated by the incubator's teams in terms of tools, best practices and processes. Thus, the corporate sponsor solely acts as a mentor, go-to-market facilitator, and VC is some cases. The team at CA found that it is probable that ideas and products from external entrepreneurs and startups might not fit to the company's overall business strategy, simply because it was not designed to, and the risks of excessively stretching the initial corporate offer is real. This approach would mainly aim to acculturate the corporate teams to a 'startup' state of mind, tools and processes, and to eventually participate in creating a pool of financially endorsed startups that are aligned with corporate values but hardly integrate further.

Further research done by the team at CA found that other companies would opt for a model 'closer to home', whether by launching a corporate accelerator themselves or a corporate intrepreneurship programme. In both cases, being closer means ideas and future businesses should be able to integrate to the corporate offer better and, as a result, make the overall process less painful. However, investments in functioning and managing costs are naturally higher than an externalised approach, and might weigh heavily on the ROI of the initiative. Costs and implications are even more engaging in the intrepreneurship model as it intends to dedicate voluntary employees on the development of new projects, full time, as well as defining processes to foster, select, fund, implement and scale ideas. Furthermore, the return of employees with unsuccessful projects might be tricky to handle should they disagree with the selection process or prefer the entrepreneurial lifestyle to their previous working habits.

Another, and rather new, model presented undeniable advantages according to CA, combining the pros of working from a distance and the possibility to preserve a strategic and operational link to the bank: the corporate startup studio. Successful startup studios such as eFounders in Paris and Finleap in Berlin have demonstrated the interest of industrialising startup creation: targeted pre-seed investments, shorter 'build' phases, a combined learning curve between startups through the support of the studio's shared resources and mutualisation of rare, key skills. CA felt that a corporate startup studio would preserve the natural advantages of the independent model and layer it with a set of undeniable unfair advantages from the bank for the future startups to be launched, such as expertise and reputation on the financial market, authorisations and certifications, and an easier access to users, amongst many others. The corporate startup studio model was approved and the creation of La Fabrique by CA was launched one month after gaining official approval. The studio very quickly defined two main missions for the future: (1) industrialising startup creation and (2) successfully hybridising startups to the bank.

in-depth and then be confronted by other teams within the bank working on related projects. The approach to such situations may be tricky to handle: times are in general shorter when working in the studio and it may reach interesting results in a faster and more efficient way. However, isolated efforts that cannot rely on the bank's advantages due to internal competition are worthless, and there is no point in sticking to an idea if there is no potential leverage to be obtained in the near future, due to divergence on 'who does what'. La Fabrique by CA has come to similar situations many times and has learnt there are only two ways out, and sticking blindly to initial thoughts is not one of them. Either you can convince the competing teams that they can work together and merge forces, or you retreat temporarily from the disputed topic until you feel you can bring it back safely to build on first results.

Therefore, delivery does not rely only on the acuteness of the idea, market fit, business model or team skills, but also on the subtle balance that is to be found with corporate teams in order to ensure a thorough and solid sponsorship from pilot phases to go-to-market.

Results

After two years of experimentation and innovation, La Fabrique by CA has launched six startups and is working on two new projects for 2021. The team has grown to 15 people, supporting the 60+ people working in the studio's startups. The studio has sold to its corporate parent its first ever startup (a financial bot advisor called Trajectoires Patrimoine en Ligne) to favour better inclusion the bank's IT systems. La Fabrique by CA also had to delay one project to ensure better sponsorship later, and agreed to turn a POC into a corporate project to integrate better with similar local initiatives in the bank's regional directions.

The studio started small, with assignments from the bank, before taking a more global approach to the market and recently launching a complete neobank, dedicated to erasing all the banking and accounting pain points in the life of individual workers. The neobank will, at the difference of all its main competitors, be able to craft joint financial services with the bank that only a well-established and experienced banking institution can provide. Hybridisation to the bank has grown to such a full alignment now that the studio spearheads the bank's peripheric innovation and acculturation to fintech.

Today the studio leads the bank's efforts on the way towards open innovation and through the BaaS revolution, providing CA with a safe space to discuss, ideate and experiment.

Learnings

When navigating within the bank for ideas, support and validation, anticipation is key: the studio is now structured to be able to work on politics and business at the same time, in order to ensure a full commitment and support for every corporate stakeholder, from top management to local branches. Though it would seem natural to go for a national implementation at every startup launch, the studio also learned that implementation can be sequenced, targeted and temporised in order to prepare a better commercialisation and penetration of the market, leveraging the right assets in the right situations and contexts.

Conveniently enough, failures and pauses in a startup studio activity does not appear to have a negative impact. The team has found that it is crucial to systematically explain the pros and cons to the team and make sure everyone understands the outcome of a project when it is stopped for any reason.

On a human resources standpoint, the spearhead position of the studio demands processes to ensure continuous learning and exploration, in order to be able to improve, pivot and reinvent on a regular basis. Two years after the launch, having a look in the rear mirror helps identifying what has been done but also what needs to change and be improved: the studio stills need to define when and how to onboard entrepreneurs as CEOs of the startups in creation (the 'build' phase). The initial model that grants the bank with 100% of the startups shares is challenging, regarding CEOs' commitment and engagement. Recruiting a CEO at the early stages of product definition might also help to engage them more; defining their own vision for product development, staffing and global strategic orientations.

The studio also learnt that agility comes at a cost: being able to accept and take advantage of an ever-shifting organisation is essential to join the team. One of the studio's missions is to try and preserve an everlasting link between the startups and the bank, no matter how much it is being stretched or crushed or pressured. The studio has taken some time to acknowledge this state of things and is now working on ways to make it easier for employees to cope with changes and gather around common, long-term goals.

Ultimately, the studio has also been working on stronger business models that do not rely too much on its corporate parent and to thrive better on their own in their market.

What's Next

In the first two years, La Fabrique by CA secured the support of all the different market divisions and subsidiaries of the bank, and proved that the studio could deliver great startups with solid products, teams and business models. Today, the corporate startup studio has to prove it can foster growth for itself and its portfolio of startups, especially working on future investments and skills development.

Now the studio needs to sort out a new bunch of hot topics, such as external investments, CEO engagement and corporate VC activities, beyond the overall challenge of sustaining scaling for the startups that have already launched.

Chapter 6
National Australia Bank Incubating Ideas

Case: QuickBiz

Executive Summary

There were concerns that National Australia Bank (NAB) was slower to market with new propositions compared to emerging competitors, particularly neo banks coming into the Australian market. The work to create the Innovation Hub was started in 2014 with the first component of the Hub being called 'NAB Labs'. While the original thinking was that the bank was under-prioritising digital investment, one finding was that the digital progress and funding were comparable to peers but fragmented and not focused on better customer outcomes. The need to accelerate innovation (versus relying on new core tech to magically provide innovation step change) was key.

The Innovation process was anchored in 12-week sprints through a Discover–Define–Validate–Iterate and Create–Transition to customer pilot sequence. Teams working on specific ideas usually consisted of an Experiment owner, a Business Analyst, a Scrum Master, User Experience expert, Customer Experience expert and Developers/Testers. A blend of agile, service experience and user experience tools were utilised within NAB Labs.

QuickBiz was the first major NAB Labs success story, the first automated SME lending decision proposition from a bank globally (some fintechs had developed similar solutions, but no major banks), delivered in early 2016, leveraging cloud accounting data and API connections.

Introductions

Do you want more details about this case? Find additional highlights from these interviews at www.howbanksinnovate.com.

Howard Silby, Chief Innovation Officer

Howard was previously the Chief Operating Officer at the Bank of New Zealand (an NAB subsidiary) and prior to that at NAB has held a variety of roles including responsibility for Business Lending, Deposits, Enterprise Risk, Chief Marketing Officer and CEO of Ubank. Howard joined NAB in late 2006 and prior to that worked in Financial Services in the UK. Howard holds an MBA from Durham University in the United Kingdom and a Master's degree in Statistics from New Zealand.

Rachel Slade, Group Executive, Personal Banking

Rachel Slade was appointed to the role of NAB's Group Executive, Personal Banking, in June 2020. Previously, she was Chief Customer Experience Officer and Executive General Manager Deposits and Transaction Services. Rachel joined NAB from Westpac at the start of 2017, where for more than 10 years she held a number of senior executive roles including leading the global transactional services business and the customer-led transformation in the retail and business bank. Rachel holds a Bachelor of Economics from Macquarie University, is a graduate of the Australian Institute of Company Directors and a graduate of the Harvard Business School's Women's Leadership Program.

Sheehan Tan, Head of Innovation

Sheehan is the Head of Innovation for NAB. Sheehan's most recent roles have focused on leading intrapreneurship at NAB for small-to-medium businesses. Prior to that, he has held roles across a wide range of disciplines including product management, credit risk, group strategy and marketing. Sheehan joined NAB in early 2008, holds a Bachelor degree with honours in Engineering and Commerce from the University of Melbourne and is a Chartered Financial Analyst.

Background

Key Figures

Total assets: A$ 800 billion
Number of customers: 4 million
Number of branches: 1,600
Number of full-time employees: 30,000
(Approximate as of 2020)

NAB is one of the four largest financial institutions in Australia. It operates as a retail and business bank in Australia and New Zealand (under the brand Bank of New Zealand, BNZ) and as a wholesale bank in major global markets. Within both Australia and New Zealand NAB is dominant in small-medium enterprise business banking and the largest business unit within the group is the Australian Business Banking division, which contributes over 40% of group revenues.

The bank is organized into five major customer-facing divisions, four of which are large in size and generate well over A$ 1 billion of revenue:

- Australian Business & Private Banking
- Australian Personal Banking
- Ubank (a smaller division comprising NAB's Australian consumer digital attacker bank)
- Corporate and Institutional Banking
- Bank of New Zealand

NAB has a Strategy and Innovation division reporting to the Group CEO, which houses the NAB group-wide Innovation and

Partnerships team. This team was brought together in 2020. Prior to 2020 Innovation was housed in a now disbanded Australian division called Customer, Products and Services, which reported to the Group CEO. The significant change in 2020 resulted in Innovation & Partnerships being combined with Strategy, M&A, Transformation and Working methods and having a Group-wide mandate for the first time.

Problem

'Before, iterative innovation was happening everywhere in the bank, which can be successful, but it must bear fruit within a short period of time. However, real transformation and disruption takes time and must be allowed to take time.'

Howard Silby, Chief Innovation Officer

The NAB Innovation Hub was launched in 2015 as a result of several key observations:

- Concerns at NAB's slower speed to market with customer propositions than emerging competitors, particularly neo banks coming into the Australian market.
- Key areas of weakness emerging in areas where 'fintech'/agile teams were creating innovative competitive solutions, especially in the area of small business and payments.
- The need to find a way of being easier to engage for fintech star-tups and disruptors where the bank chose to partner with them.
- Frustration that business and technology were not collaborating well and increasing Board level anxiety about the cost and com-plexity of large WIP technology programmes seeking to 'indus-trialise' the banks technology platform.
- A lack of innovation/digital innovation proof points in recent years, in part due to the impact of one specific very large core systems replacement programme (the 'Next Gen' programme)

that had led to resource scarcity in other areas of the bank and an over-reliance on the new core system to deliver enterprise level innovation.

- An inability to share innovation across different parts of the bank, including leveraging innovation being developed in UBank into the core brand.
- The desire for an enterprise-wide innovation capability owned by the board and exec team rather than control residing with one particular executive.
- The need to be culturally ready to leverage the possibilities of new technology, whether delivered through the core systems activity or other technology that emerged.

The work to create the Innovation Hub was started in 2014. While the original thinking was that the bank was under-prioritising digital investment, one finding was that the digital progress and funding was comparable to peers but fragmented and not focused on better customer outcomes. The need to accelerate innovation (versus rely on new core tech to magically provide innovation step change) was key.

As the principal challenge became refined from 'how do we accelerate digital' to 'how do we build a process to accelerate innovation' NAB considered a variety of options:

- Distributed models
- Outsourcing
- Pure M&A (acquisition of an innovation engine/digital incubator)
- Alliances and partnerships

Several models were considered to try and increase innovation cadence in the bank. The model chosen was a hybrid of the above and reflected the need to have something impactful, effective, internally owned, yet different to the core, and able to operate very differently.

There was a strong sense amongst the NAB executive that banks were under increasing attack from traditional competitors plus a proliferation of new entrants who think, behave and progress in a very different way to existing financial services business models. The central recognition was that in this new world, the customer is in control and only organisations that can adapt through sensing and shaping customer expectations will thrive. To win, NAB determined it must give customers an experience that creates an emotional connection with a distinct value proposition.

As a result, the Innovation Hub began with a couple of key components that stood it in good stead, a relentless focus on the customer and a willingness to separate its technology funding and free-up technology resources and constraints. This latter point proved to be both a benefit and a source of difficulty in later years but did allow for the successful quick implementation of a range of propositions.

Solution

'We want to build in-house, vs partner, when we want the end result to be a core capability, something that we want to be known for.'

Sheehan Tan, Head of Innovation

The innovation hub assembled a cross-functional group of individuals to allow disruptive innovation to go to market quickly and efficiently and to 'change the way the bank changes'.

Key elements of the NAB Labs approach included the use of:

- Cross-functional teams
- Human-centred design
- Agile methods
- Partners, often introduced or met via the NAB Ventures arm of the Innovation hub
- Separately empowered technology resource

The Innovation process was anchored in 12-week sprints through a Discover–Define–Validate–Iterate and Create–Transition to customer pilot sequence. Teams working on specific ideas usually consisted of an Experiment Owner, a Business Analyst, a Scrum Master, User Experience expert, Customer Experience expert and Developers/Testers. A blend of agile, service experience and user experience tools were utilised within NAB Labs. The use of agile was relatively new to NAB at the time NAB Labs began.

The service design focus on ensuring services and strategies were desirable, feasible and viable and was also an important component in the NAB Labs approach, as was the use of user experience methodologies. The primary goal of user experience is to uncover a thorough understanding of users, their needs, their abilities, their limitations and their priorities and to design and bring to life the outcomes of research.

The brand 'NAB Labs' was used to describe the Innovation activity and process and it gained widespread recognition internally.

Some of the original observations and Board concerns that led to the creation of the Innovation hub did end up being implemented in ways that changed over time. The desire for an enterprise-wide innovation capability rather than control residing with one particular executive, resulted in the Innovation Hub initially being located in an independent Executive role reporting to the Group CEO. However, at a later stage the Innovation Hub did end up within one division, the Australian Customer, Products and Services division.

The innovation hub ultimately comprised two components: initially NAB Labs, a dedicated team to build, test and trial new value propositions and new ways of working, and then NAB Ventures, an innovation fund that invested in Australian and offshore startups including mobile platforms, payments and data analytics companies. NAB Ventures began in early 2016.

Together these two teams formed the key parts of the NAB Innovation Hub from 2016 onward, which was intended to bring new product and service solutions faster to market for customers, in many cases leveraging the partnerships and ideas that the Ventures part of the team had brought forward. NAB Labs was the key part of the innovation hub that was focused on the rapid experimentation and commercialisation of customer-led innovation. Primarily driven by human-centred design, NAB Labs investigated current challenges the bank faced to identify, prototype and iteratively deliver solutions.

The introduction of agile, service and user experience methodologies including human-centred design had a lasting impact on NAB, and to an extent the 'change the way we change' objective of the Innovation Hub had a longer legacy than the specific deliverables that resulted from the Innovation Hub, which will be discussed in the next section.

The NAB Innovation Hub remained in this form until early 2020 when the two parts of the Innovation Hub were brought together under a new Chief Innovation Officer, relocated alongside the Strategy, M&A, Transformation and Working methods teams and as per the original intention in 2015, was given a Group-wide mandate to undertake Innovation for all parts of the NAB Group including the Bank of New Zealand and Ubank.

Delivery

'I think the key to getting better at anything is to be constantly constructively dissatisfied and adopting a learning mindset – win or learn!'

Rachel Slade, Group Executive, Personal Banking

During 2016 to 2019 NAB Labs delivered over 20 in-market propositions. There were two significant successes that arose from the Innovation Hub, 'QuickBiz' and 'Slyp', which had a material impact on the Australian market.

QuickBiz was the first major NAB Labs success story, the first automated SME lending decision proposition from a bank globally (some fintechs had developed similar solutions, but no major banks), delivered in early 2016, leveraging cloud accounting data and API connections.

It became a very significant success, accounting for over half of small business lending by the NAB small business division, and has since been replicated by competitors.

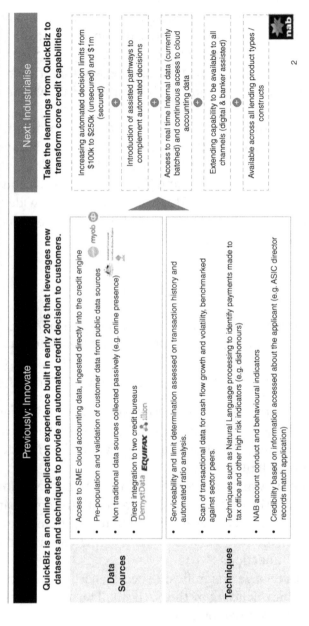

SME CREDIT DECISIONING: NAB 2016-17 INNOVATION THROUGH 'QUICKBIZ'

Previously: Innovate

QuickBiz is an online application experience built in early 2016 that leverages new datasets and techniques to provide an automated credit decision to customers.

Data Sources

- Access to SME cloud accounting data, ingested directly into the credit engine
- Pre-population and validation of customer data from public data sources
- Non traditional data sources collected passively (e.g. online presence)
- Direct integration to two credit bureaus DemystData EQUIFAX illion

Techniques

- Serviceability and limit determination assessed on transaction history and automated ratio analysis.
- Scan of transactional data for cash flow growth and volatility, benchmarked against sector peers.
- Techniques such as Natural Language processing to identify payments made to tax office and other high risk indicators (e.g. dishonours)
- NAB account conduct and behavioural indicators
- Credibility based on information accessed about the applicant (e.g. ASIC director records match application)

Next: Industrialise

Take the learnings from QuickBiz to transform core credit capabilities

- Increasing automated decision limits from $100k to $250k (unsecured) and $1m (secured)
- Introduction of assisted pathways to complement automated decisions
- Access to real time internal data (currently batched) and continuous access to cloud accounting data
- Extending capability to be available to all channels (digital & banker assisted)
- Available across all lending product types / constructs

2

Quickbiz was built and launched as an MVP in customers' hands over a 14-week period, and proved the use of disparate partners. One such partner was DeMyst data, based out of New York, as well as cross-functional business and technology teams. The proposition initially offered SME customers unsecured amortising loans, the full application and approval process taking less than 20 minutes, with cash received the next day. The proposition was iterated throughout 2016 and 2017 before the delivery of new customer features slowed and focus turned to integrating the proposition more into NAB's core technology platforms.

'Slyp', a digital receipting solution is also a NAB Innovation Hub success story, this time built entirely outside of NAB. The idea and software was already trialled in multiple iterations with NAB in 2017 and the NAB became one of the early adopters of Slyp's white-labelled software product when it came to market in 2019. To be successful Slyp had to be bank agnostic, so an unusual feature of the Slyp success story is that the corporate Venture companies, both NAB and a rival bank Westpac, became seed funders for Slyp in 2018 (NAB Ventures would not normally participate in a seed round) and collaboration with other banks is in this case essential to the marketplace success of Slyp.

NAB continues to benefit, however, from its early involvement with Slyp, including more recently in 2020 being the first bank to deliver full Slyp integration into its banking app.

A number of very positive features resulted from the introduction of the Innovation Hub at NAB:

- A customer-problem led approach.
- Rooted in rich customer insights.
- Experiment based approach to design a solution or deliver the desired outcome.
- Rapid stage gate approach to progress or kill initiatives.
- Collaborative multidisciplinary approach to problem solving, around CX, UX, Tech and Business coming together to find the right solution.
- Getting an answer/view with a light touch investment.
- Speed to arrive at a decision.

nabventures

NABV PORTFOLIO SERVICES
SUCCESS STORIES – Slyp

TA6
8.2

COMPANY PROFILE

Slyp is a Sydney-based **digital receipting company**, developing technology to issue receipts from the Point of Sale (PoS) software directly into the consumers banking app.

The digital receipt captures **basket level data** that can be used to fuel **analytics** and **insights** for banks and merchants. As the receipt is linked to a unique card, offers and rewards can be claimed seamlessly.

First successful integration into the **NAB mobile banking app** went live in **October 2019.**

DEAL STRUCTURE

Date of investment: April 2018

NAB Ventures led Slyp's **A$2m Seed funding** round, alongside Reinventure in 2018.

INTEGRATION DESCRIPTION

Date of first pilot: October 2019 (1.5 years after NAB Ventures investment)

Slyp and NAB have been integrating NAB Ventures portfolio company's solution into the NAB banking app with the goal of allowing NAB customers to receive their **receipts digitally in-app** creating a **frictionless experience.**

Pilot divided into 3 phases:
- **Phase 1** *(live from October 2019)*: Slyp receipts generated through OCR applied to photos taken by NAB customers;
- **Phase 2** *(live from September 2020)*: Slyp Smart receipts generated in-app when purchasing from accredited merchants;
- **Phase 3** (date *TBD*): Inclusion of loyalty/reward programs in-app.

STRATEGIC RATIONALE

PORTFOLIO COMPANY	NAB
• Test Slyp's solution and develop a **solid use case** with NAB; • Strengthen Slyp's solution for **potential future integrations** • Tap into **NAB's business customers** segment	• Digital receipts will improve **user experience** for NAB customers and increase engagement within the NAB app • Form the basis for **next phase** of integration

STRATEGIC IMPACT

PORTFOLIO COMPANY	NAB
• Built solid foundations to proceed to **phase 3** of integration • Slyp solution proven **effective**	• Improved **user experience** for NAB cutomers • Increased **engagement** within the NAB app

FUTURE OPPORTUNITIES

• **Loyalty program:** Include loyalty programs in NAB app to manage rewards, increase customer loyalty and collect more personalised data

NOT EXHAUSTIVE

MAIN STAKEHOLDERS

Slyp   PODIUM

However, a number of problems emerged with the NAB Labs approach, leading to the changes of 2020:

- NAB Labs and NAB Ventures were too separate, although Slyp was a major success, it was rare that NAB Labs incubated a proposition from a Ventures partner.
- Eventually there were too many 'so-so' deliverables from NAB Labs, not enough game changers that 'solve our most pressing problems'.
- NAB Labs lost its aura as a magnet for internal talent, and an internal perception arose that the team was too big and working on too many things that did not make a sufficient difference. This may have been more perception than reality but in a resource constrained environment, 'large' teams become easy targets.
- NAB Labs and NAB Ventures became too separate from Group Strategy and Group Development, so that ideas and partnerships and acquisitions did not serve the priority areas of group strategy.
- The separate technology used by the Innovation Hub became a problem for future integration and scaling back into the bank. Ultimately technology resources were reduced in the Innovation Hub such that propositions became in danger of being too close to 'PR' showcases rather than game-changing customer propositions with rapid paths to scale.

Results

Of the nine largest innovations incubated by NAB Labs in 2016–2019, these are the results:

- **Initiative A.** Established leadership for NAB in a particular area, but unclear if this will be sustained.
- **Initiative B.** Still very delicately positioned, may create a competitive advantage but yet to be proven.
- **Initiative C.** Failed.

- **Initiative D.** Mostly failed.
- **Initiative E.** Moderate impact, more of a PR gimmick.
- **Initiative F.** Had some impact but no longer in the market.
- **Initiative G.** Established leadership for NAB in a particular area, but unclear if this will be sustained.

The other two initiatives were 'Quickbiz' and 'Slyp'. This would suggest at least a quarter still have their full potential yet to be assessed, up to a quarter have definitively failed, up to a quarter had a limited impact and up to a quarter are having a significant impact.

In addition to the specific deliverables of the Innovation Hub incubations, there have undoubtedly been a range of softer benefits from the Innovation hub activity. This included a lasting culture of human-centred design, service design and business awareness and utilisation of agile methodologies.

Learnings

The learnings from this first leg of the Innovation Hub at NAB, and approaches by its NZ subsidiary the Bank of New Zealand, can be summarised in the following ways:

- Several cultural wins helped usher in Human Centred Design across NAB.
- Self-contained technology resources delivered successful real customer propositions.
- However, some successful propositions ended up having to be 'rebuilt'.
- When technology resources were re-pointed to the Core bank, innovation activity lost its 'self-reliance' and was de-prioritised.
- Subsequent experimental playgrounds/sandboxes became too isolated from the core platforms and thus sometimes became PR showcases rather than anything scalable/real.
- The venture fund approach is good for exposure to technology and startups.

- Exploration of new partners was often too slow.
- Separate startup mentality great for talent acquisition.
- Ideas too 'separate/outside Financial Services' can quickly lose Executive support.

Whilst there are many learning points here represented as 'areas for improvement' it is undeniably true that the introduction of the Innovation Hub has had a lasting impact on NAB. There is strong clarity and alignment among the NAB senior executives on the innovation approach going forward.

What's Next

The collective learnings from the first five years of the Innovation Hub at NAB have been distilled into a new approach to innovation at NAB from 2020 onwards. The central intention of the two main parts of the original Innovation Hub, NAB Labs and NAB Ventures remain, although branding is likely to change and NAB Labs is no longer used as an internal brand, following the dissipation of the team. Resources dedicated to the incubation of ideas have been consolidated and given priority once again, and the two parts of the Innovation hub have been brought together under a new Chief Innovation Officer, relocated alongside the Strategy, M&A, Transformation and Working methods. The team has been given a group-wide mandate to undertake Innovation for all parts of the NAB Group, including the Bank of New Zealand and Ubank.

There are 12 hallmarks in all of the re-booted approaches to Innovation from 2020 onward:

- A focus on improving the core bank and taking the bank forward in leaps, but not pursuing ideas too separate from the Financial Services core.
- The team operates as a ring-fenced resource for 'horizon 2 or 3' ideas that are not just immediately adjacent or iterative to what the business is already doing.

- Starting with the customer not the partner or venture company, use market scanning functions to drive ideas. Focus on desirability and then ensuring propositions are feasible and commercially viable.
- Determining the right vehicle for validating propositions in-market quickly, including using Partners or where relevant actually deliver a POC or Incubation with real customers, including the live technology solution.
- Aligned to group strategy, operating as a Group function on priorities across the Group and avoiding any perception of being aligned to certain business lines or functional areas.
- Working on an agreed target number of innovations and outcomes with the CEO.
- Working in agreed Innovation opportunity spaces, having a clear innovation thesis agreed with senior executives, and a governance process.
- Developing a standardised repeatable process with a business sponsor commitment at go/no-go points.
- Utilising agile working methods and innovative working approaches.
- Staying close to the technology team innovation centre/architecture lab, as many innovation insights and topics inevitably require a deep understanding of currents in technology.
- Developing known fast-paths in key areas; Privacy, Conduct, Brand, Procurement and Technology (including Security).
- Developing purpose-built innovation components within technology (innovation at the 'edge' not completely separate, but not reliant on core technology either) and more collaboration with technology rather than parallel or separate innovation builds.

The final point is particularly important as the dissipation of the NAB Labs approach in part was due to the relationship between the core technology areas of the bank and 'innovation', which had become too separate. The organisational attitude and relationship between 'technology' and 'innovation' in many ways has been critical to the evolution of the Innovation Hub at NAB through various phases.

Chapter 7
Citi
Building In-house, Managing In house

Case: Spring by Citi

Executive Summary

The massive growth in e-commerce has created opportunities for companies to grow their businesses into new channels, consumer bases and geographies.

However, to partake in e-commerce, businesses needed to develop an online payments strategy around the many paths to market. Companies invested considerable time and resources to understand the complex, fragmented and rapidly evolving world of online payments in order to bring their businesses online. The complexity of the payments landscape and evolving nature of the online world created an opportunity for innovation, differentiation and simplification, an opportunity that Citi launched a solution for.

To address the needs of its clients, Citi's Treasury and Trade Solutions (TTS) business launched Spring by Citi^{SM}, a payment processing solution that integrates a wide range of payment methods with back-office treasury management systems and processes. Spring by Citi simplifies the complexities of accepting online payments by offering a holistic solution from a single provider.

Spring by Citi was developed and launched in record time compared to other initiatives in the bank, going from ideation to launch in 18 months by using newer development processes including design thinking and agile development methodology.

Introductions

Do you want more details about this case? Find additional highlights from these interviews at www.howbanksinnovate.com.

Manish Kohli, Global Head, Payments and Receivables, Treasury and Trade Solutions

Manish leads Citi's Institutional Payments and Receivables business globally, one of the pillars of Citi's Treasury and Trade Solutions

(TTS) division. TTS offers comprehensive solutions for Corporate, Public Sector and FI clients to enable growth and progress, drive operating efficiencies and improve working capital management. Manish is currently Citi's PAYCO Board member at The Clearing House (TCH), sits on the Payment Risk Committee of the Federal Reserve Bank of New York and represents Citi on SWIFT's gpi vision group.

Anupam Sinha, Managing Director, Domestic Payments and Receivables, Treasury and Trade Solutions

Anupam has more than 20 years' experience in transaction banking. Anupam is responsible for the business globally, including overseeing Citi's direct access to 250+ clearing houses. In addition to Spring by Citi, Anupam is also responsible for rolling out Instant Payments globally to future proof Citi's payment network. Anupam has been active in the payments industry and regularly participates at industry panel discussions. He has been on the founding board of directors of the UK Faster Payments scheme, one of the first instant payments schemes globally.

Rishi Patel, Global Head of Product, Spring

Rishi has been with Citi for over 15 years in roles across Technology Infrastructure, Program Management and Business Analysis & Product Management. Rishi has a track record of product delivery, including the launch of Citi® Virtual Accounts and the partnership with HighRadius to launch Citi® Smart Match. Rishi led the research and strategy around Citi's entering into the Consumer Payments space, becoming Global Head of Product for the new business line in early 2019. Rishi has a BSc in Computer Science & e-Business from Loughborough University, England.

Arlene Ennis, Global Technology Head for Spring

Arlene is leading the technology delivery for the Spring by Citi Initiative within Citi. Prior to this, she had extensive experience running large complex IT Programs and Projects and managing large global teams. She is now responsible for a global team of 40+ people, creating a 'best in class' solution for processing consumer to business, e-Commerce transactions for global institutional clients. Arlene has 18+ years of Financial Services Experience, a BSc in Software Engineering and holds an MBA from Dublin City University, Ireland.

Background

Key figures

Total assets: $1.95 trillion
Number of customers: 200 million
Number of branches: 2,300
Number of full-time employees: 200,000
(Approximate as of 2020)

Citi was formed by a business combination of Citicorp and Travelers Group in 1998 and is today the third largest bank in the US and one of the 10 largest in the world, operating across 160 markets. As a global bank for consumers, corporations, governments and institutions, Citi provides its client base with a broad range of financial products and services, including consumer banking and credit, corporate and investment banking, securities brokerage, transaction services, and wealth management.

Treasury and Trade Solutions (TTS), a business within Citi's Institutional Clients Group, enables its clients by providing an integrated suite and tailored cash management and trade finance services to multinational corporations, financial institutions and public sector organisations across the globe. Although TTS offers a comprehensive range of digitally enabled treasury, trade and liquidity management solutions to its client base, it did not offer its client base e-commerce solutions for online payments acceptance.

Problem

By 2023, global e-commerce sales to consumers are expected to reach $6.5 trillion and account for 22% of global retail sales. Given the tremendous opportunity, digital commerce is becoming core to the growth strategy of businesses across many industries, from services to asset-heavy sectors. Industry research estimates that by 2025, about one third of global economic activity could resolve into digital platforms that cater to consumers and businesses.

This shifting paradigm is causing many companies with primarily business-to-business distribution models to deploy e-commerce strategies, creating a new sales channel and therefore revenue opportunity, across the globe. When pivoting to direct-to-consumer sales models, companies have many paths to market and must develop a strategy for accepting online payments, a highly complex and rapidly evolving landscape. Some companies go direct-to-consumer by selling their products on an online marketplace, a solution that requires less direct investment but lessens the control of user experience and product margins. Other companies go direct-to-consumer by developing their own webstore, giving them full control over the user experience, product fulfillment and online payment strategy.

As consumer expectations evolve and frictionless digital experiences become paramount to customer satisfaction, companies already in the world of e-commerce currently invest significant time and resources to ensure their platforms are locally relevant and have access to the latest technologies. For multinational companies operating online in multiple geographies, their businesses must factor in varying local regulations, market practices and consumer preferences. The complexity of the payments landscape and evolving nature of the online world creates an opportunity for innovation, differentiation and simplification, an opportunity that Citi decided to launch a solution for.

Citi recognised a need where their clients were looking for a payments solution to facilitate their global commerce, empowering them to exist in a dynamic and digital environment. The need was to be able to collect using consumer-facing payment methods like cards and wallets in a globally consistent manner and something that was seamlessly integrated with their e-commerce website or App.

Their strategy was underpinned by the following imperatives:

- **A defensive strategy.** The strength of their network with presence in 95+ markets and direct access to 250+ clearing houses needs to be continuously bolstered with solutions to ensure they remain their client's preferred cash management bank. The team saw the development of the Consumer Payments proposition as one such solution they needed to invest in.
- **An offensive growth strategy.** They needed to extend the share of the wallet by attracting new client flows, in this case enabling their e-commerce business, a significant growth opportunity.

A key client problem in this space was the need to use many different providers and having to piece together the solutions they were seeking due to the absence of a truly global provider. This could be an opportunity given Citi's past track record of having done this once before in the corporate payments space, where Citi enabled clients to centralise their payment operations globally.

A typical approach for banks is to leverage as much of existing infrastructure and operating model as possible to minimise costs. However, as Citi was not in the online payments business, the team quickly knew that such an approach would introduce complexity and constrain the ambitions of launching with scale and differentiation. Instead, Citi needed to take a blank-canvas approach to the challenge of designing and building the new proposition whilst also obtaining the necessary product, legal, compliance and regulatory approvals in order to launch.

Solution

'What we have done well over the past few years is to embed innovation across our organisation: all departments, all colleagues. Innovation is no longer the preserve of our Labs or innovation teams.'

Manish Kohli, Global Head, Payments and Receivables,
Treasury and Trade Solutions

In March of 2019, the bank announced that it was developing a new business line for consumers to make digital payments to institutions. This was part of TTS's overall strategy to enable digital commerce for clients and extend its significant presence and capabilities beyond the wholesale payments space. The new solution would enable Citi's clients to accept online payments from consumers in a wide range of payment methods, including credit and debit cards, e-wallets and bank transfers. This streamlined solution would make payments ubiquitous for both consumers and online companies, a need in the market. Payment ubiquity was not the only market need, as online companies also lacked transparency and visibility into reporting and wanted expedited funds settlement and integration with their wider cash management structures. Citi's new business would deliver value across companies' organisations by bringing together the varying needs of corporate treasury, e-commerce teams and commercial teams.

One of the major challenges Citi faced in starting up this new business was introducing the solution to the marketplace. In short, corporate buying centres did not know that Citi offered the solution and Citi was new to the landscape. This created challenges when it came to selling the solution. E-commerce and other business teams were more familiar with fintechs, which made it considerably more difficult to compete. To meet these challenges, the bank had to train its sales people on a whole new solution, which required a new way of selling. A reimagined sales tool kit was created to address the needs of the sales team and a Spring by Citi Academy training programme was put in place to ensure their sales force could drive the business effectively. This is an ongoing effort, as they strive to become a recognised leader in the space.

In terms of the product launch itself, Citi approached the development of the new business line differently than other product launches by using design-thinking techniques and adopting a progressive marketing strategy, which enabled the bank to achieve speed to market and move with agility. Design thinking centred around deeply understanding and defining client needs, ideating and validating possible solutions, and revising and iterating based upon the results. This approach enabled Citi to understand the specific capabilities the solution should comprise and that the power of branding could create a platform for marketing the solution to companies that would not traditionally consider Citi as a player in this space.

The ambition was to create recognition, trust and inspire both internal and external stakeholders with the possibilities this solution represented for Citi. In October of 2019, Citi introduced the new business line as Spring by Citi, demonstrating the bank's fresh thinking. Spring, a dynamic and multifaceted word, was chosen as the business line's name to signify a leap forward, elasticity and new beginnings.

Spring by Citi was launched in June of 2020 and simplifies the complexity of accepting online payments by driving secure and seamless payment processing and by balancing the objectives of frictionless user experiences with risk mitigation. The solution provides a centralised way for online businesses to accept online payments, a critical capability in today's increasingly global and digital world. This solution, provided under a single contract with Citi, includes full merchant acquiring services, funds settlement with embedded foreign exchange and increased transparency to automate reconciliation.

Delivery

'Our in-house Labs team brought together those within the bank with the most relevant experience and we also used external consultancies to speed up the ideation and validation phase.'

Arlene Ennis, Global Technology Head for Spring by Citi

The bank set out to develop the best consumer payments proposition in the market. In doing so, the team analysed whether to put together a referral arrangement, complete an acquisition, or build around existing assets such as Cash Management and Foreign Exchange (FX) by partnering with external providers. Initially, the team chose to develop and build upon the power of Citi's network, its local branch presence, and enter into partnerships with market-leading players, leveraging their technology and expertise to achieve speed to market.

However, it quickly became apparent that referring all credit card processing and acquiring on behalf of Citi would not meet the rigorous requirements around client experience and the bank's need for adequate control over the solution. Referring would create counterparty exposure for clients, which was deemed unacceptable. As a result, TTS recognised the need to include merchant acquiring in its Spring by Citi product.

The bank faced the challenge of creating an entirely new credit card processing function within the bank, which meant creating a new operating model with a new set of onboarding processes, operations, service processes and policies. In order to secure senior management approval, a strong business case was put forward. After considerable discussion, it was decided to move forward so as to best address client needs.

One of the earliest challenges in moving forward was how to advance the solution with limited subject matter expertise. The bank understood that there were many unknown unknowns, which would require hiring new personnel expeditiously and with the right mindset for this new business. Due to their global scale, finding people with the right fit was paramount. This effort is ongoing as Citi seeks to ensure that the ambition of this business is fulfilled.

The bank's ability to adapt has been instrumental to progress this venture. To achieve the stated ends, the team implemented a very structured development methodology to detail tasks across the entire lifecycle of product development from ideation to launch.

From a product development perspective, Citi designed the solution using development methodologies new to the bank and focused on creating openness in a new architecture that could evolve as the requirements evolved, providing room for learnings and new requirements. The agile development methodology featured compressed build times, meaning Citi could quickly move from design to development, analyse each release, reap learnings, and shift direction as necessary. Citi broke down silos and worked as an integrated team across product management, technology and operations to develop user stories that lead to the rapid build out of Spring by Citi's core infrastructure. The joint ownership of responsibilities across the organisation provided for deep collaboration, diversity of thought and kept client needs at the heart of the solution.

Spring by Citi harnesses partner technology to leverage an established payment gateway, card-processing platform and access to local payment methods. When combined, these technologies provide secure and streamlined access to the world of online payments. As Citi developed the new core infrastructure and integrated with the partner technology, the team took a differentiated approach to perform extensive end-to-end testing of the new solution. Citi hired a consultant specialised in the payments industry to function as a new online business looking to accept online payments. The consultant was on-boarded to Spring by Citi as a test client and fully integrated with the solution, validating the new technology development. In addition, this approach allowed Citi to measure the client and consumer experience that was created, a key focus for the bank.

Results

'We knew we had to build something on our own as this would not be something sitting to the side, on one shelf, but rather be right in the core of our offering if we take a 10–15 year view.'

Anupam Sinha, Managing Director, Domestic Payments
and Receivables, Treasury and Trade Solutions

Treasury and Trade solutions saw the development of an end-to-end consumer payments proposition as a tremendous opportunity, given that clients increasingly look at transaction services as a continuum, from their receivables, to bank account structures and liquidity, to disbursements globally. Spring by Citi was developed and launched in 18 months, a record for the bank for a project of this scale.

Citi has added merchant acquiring as a new business line in the TTS product portfolio, thanks to the use of agile development methods, creating a next-generation technology stack.

Initially, Citi set its sights on going live in 10 plus countries by the end of 2020. However, the complexity of adding the merchant acquiring business affected this plan. The rollout subsequently has been scaled back to four countries with the goal of introducing more countries in the future.

The solution is live in the US, UK, Canada and Mexico, supporting payment processing for the largest card networks globally. During the first month of going to market, Citi won its first client. The client was on-boarded to Spring by Citi and was up and running in under 30 days, meeting their expedited timelines to accept online payments.

The solution supports clients with a frictionless on-boarding experience based on known industry pain points and is tailored to the clients' specific use-case. This powerful solution provides client value by:

- Simplifying relationship management that spans the payment gateway, card acquiring, alternative payment methods and settlement needs, which is all in one, with a sole provider.

- Increasing transparency across the lifecycle of payments, providing automated reconciliation activities and increased efficiency.
- Integrating with client's cash management solutions, from liquidity management to disbursements and optimising working capital.
- Providing extensive local market knowledge and on-the-ground experience.

Learnings

'One of the key learnings was that in an effort to create a more client centric proposition which incorporates full-service merchant acquiring, we did not factor the impact to project timelines and ultimately delivered less markets than originally expected. This was acceptable during the formative years of the new business but something that requires more effective planning in subsequent years as we scale and meet client and market expectations from a live business.'

Rishi Patel, Global Head of Product, Spring by Citi

In launching Spring by Citi, the bank moved with agility to design, validate and build a solution that solves client needs in a rapidly evolving space. To enable speed to market, the Spring by Citi team harnessed considerable hidden assets and established new partnerships. The team tackled challenges along the way by bringing the entire organisation along on the journey, including Risk, Compliance, Finance, Legal, and other functions, shifting mindsets and streamlining governance.

As TTS validated the solution design with clients, feedback centred on a number of considerations. Given the criticality of consumer payments flows, counterparty exposure was a key focus for clients and they wanted a relationship with Citi and Citi only. This feedback, coupled with the opportunity to provide additional value to their clients, made TTS pivot their initial strategy to incorporate full merchant acquiring into the proposition. This entailed working with the card networks and internal functions to extend existing issuing licenses with card acquiring. This change in approach, which was initially met with reservations within the bank due to the introduction of additional complexity, is enabling TTS to further differentiate its proposition. Citi has put processes in place to manage for this.

The early successes of Spring by Citi proved the solution is one that can be put at the centre of Citi's transaction banking business to take the firm further towards a future of supporting hyper-connected ecosystems with fully integrated banking products for consumers and online businesses alike.

What's Next

The business has plans to move from a 'startup' like business, to a scaled organisation, to a truly differentiated proposition. The plans are based upon four key pillars that are underpinned by Citi's investment in talent:

- **Geographic expansion,** expanding the solution to over 30 markets across the globe within the next few years, so that online businesses can transact like a local on a global scale.
- **Payment ubiquity,** incorporating the most popular local payment methods in each market, to extend payment ubiquity, or optionality, so consumers can pay in their preferred payment method and online businesses can drive sales conversion.
- **Product capabilities,** enriching product capabilities, with a focus on technologies that remove friction and optimise processes across the end-to-end solution offering.
- **Client experience,** enhancing and adapting the client experience model as the payments landscape continues to evolve with new technology, payment methods and local regulations.

Chapter 8
Bank of America
Building In-house, Managing In house

Case: Erica

BANK OF AMERICA

Executive Summary

Advances in voice technology and artificial intelligence have opened new possibilities for delivering a more personalised, convenient customer experience. Identifying a growing desire among customers for a solution that anticipates their needs and helps them reach their financial goals, Bank of America (BofA) decided to create a tool that employs AI, predictive analytics and natural language understanding.

In 2018 they launched Erica, a virtual financial assistant and personal financial tool. Its key differentiator is its ability to deliver personalised, proactive and predictive insights and guidance to help clients optimise cash flow and budgeting, avoid surprises and fees, maximise savings opportunities and get the most out of their banking relationship.

Erica was developed as part of a collaboration between the digital banking business and technology teams in a close, iterative and agile process. The core platform was created and retail banking capabilities were enabled in conversational mode in just one year.

Because Erica was developed primarily in-house by BofA technologists, the bank has accumulated 44 granted and pending patents related to the solution. This proprietary technology gives the bank a foundation for future innovations.

As of Q4 of 2020, Erica had 17 million active users, adding 500,000 new users every month. Erica processed over 100 million requests in 12 months and 80%+ of users report that the virtual assistant meets/exceeds their expectations.

Introductions

Do you want more details about this case? Find additional highlights from these interviews at www.howbanksinnovate.com.

Aditya Bhasin, Head of Consumer, Small Business, Wealth Management and Employee Experience Technology Teams

Aditya's team is responsible for designing and delivering technology for Consumer, Small Business and Wealth Management clients in the United States, through Bank of America's online and mobile banking apps as well as in financial centres and in Merrill and Private Bank offices. Aditya also leads the company's global technology strategy for employee-facing platforms. His team drives the evolution of software delivery methodologies, promotes agile development practices and sets architecture standards company-wide, as well as identifying partnerships that connect the bank to the emerging technology ecosystem and working with startups to deliver innovations for clients.

Christian Kitchell, Head of Erica & AI Solutions and Chief Digital Executive, Private Bank

As head of the Erica & AI Solutions group, Christian and his leadership team oversee all facets of platform vision, strategy, development, operational management and execution, working alongside partners in technology, analytics and across the organisation. He also leads digital servicing platforms, including IVR, chat and consumer agent desktop functionality, and serves as the Chief Digital Executive for Bank of America's Private Bank, overseeing client platforms strategy and execution.

Hari Gopalkrishnan, Client Facing Platforms Technology Executive

Hari leads the development of the next generation of integrated technology solutions for the company's Consumer and Wealth Management client-facing channels. He also manages the bank's websites and e-Commerce initiatives. Hari is responsible for the technology that drives client-facing platforms and channels across Consumer, Small Business & Wealth Management Technology. This includes, among many areas of the bank's, Global Wealth and Investment Management, Contact Centre and Voice Technology and Technology Partnership Development.

Background

Key Figures

Total assets: $2.4 trillion
Number of customers: 66 million
Number of branches: 4,300
Number of full-time employees: 212,000
(Approximate as of 2020)

Bank of America (BofA) is the second largest bank in the United States and one of the 10 largest in the world, operating across 35 countries. The bank is organised in eight lines of business:

- **Retail**, serves mass market US consumers.
- **Preferred**, provides banking and investment solutions to mass affluent US consumers with $50K to $250K in investable assets, as well as cash management, lending and investment solutions to entrepreneurs and small businesses with revenue of up to $5 million.
- **Merrill Lynch Wealth Management**, serves clients across the wealth spectrum, from those with $250,000 of investable assets to the ultra-high net worth.
- **Private Bank**, investment and wealth management solutions to ultra-high net worth clients with investable assets of more than $3 million.
- **Business Banking**, financial advice and solutions, including credit, treasury, trade, foreign exchange, equipment finance and merchant services, to small and mid-sized US companies with annual revenues of $5 million to $50 million.
- **Global Commercial Banking**, as above but middle market companies with revenues of $50 million to $2 billion across all major industries.
- **Global Corporate & Investment Banking**, as above but for clients with >$2 billion including municipalities and government agencies.
- **Global Markets**, provides services across the world's debt, equity, commodity and foreign exchange markets.

Rather than having an innovation lab, BofA believes innovation is all employees' responsibility. The bank's annual technology and operations budget is $10 billion; more than $3 billion of that goes to new technology initiatives each year, $35 billion dollars over the last 10 years. The bank's 2020 patent portfolio consisted of more than

4,400 patents granted or applied for, reflecting the work of more than 5,800 inventors based in 42 US states and 13 countries.

Problem

'People don't live to bank and not everyone embraces technology in a consistent manner. Our challenge is to make sure we design solutions that make it so easy for a client to engage with us, in a manner that is comfortable to them, that they find themselves financially empowered by the capabilities we provide.'

Hari Gopalkrishnan, Client Facing Platforms
Technology Executive

Whilst the bank's 66 million Consumer Banking clients are extremely diverse, they generally have three expectations from the bank:

- They want everyday banking to be easy and effortless.
- They want the bank to be there when they really need it.
- They want personalised help in reaching their financial goals.

The challenge is how to evolve your banking services to always meet those expectations. In that sense, banking is no different from any other customer experience in the digital era. Customers want simplicity in their transactions, self-serve when possible. As such, BofA organises its business around the customer and their journeys. 'Simple' 30 years ago was an ATM. Today, it is mobile and tomorrow it may be 'know what I need, before I ask'. However, there will always be a need to support clients through one-to-one personal interaction for more complicated needs. Bank employees will shift from processing transactions to helping clients with their most complex needs. BofA built their 'High Tech, High Touch' strategy around those points.

Advances in voice technology and consumer-facing artificial intelligence have opened new possibilities for delivering a more personalised, convenient customer experience. According to a 2018 BofA report, consumers were increasingly embracing artificial intelligence solutions. Nearly two in five respondents said they use or would use AI and 91% of AI users were comfortable with AI performing a variety of financial activities, including identifying unusual account activity, scheduling appointments, making bill payments and providing proactive alerts.

To meet the growing desire among customers for a solution that anticipates their needs and helps them reach their financial goals, BofA created a tool that employs the latest technology in AI, predictive analytics and natural language understanding.

The bank defined a list of problems they wanted to address in the process:

- Help customers achieve greater convenience and control in managing their finances.
- Offer a solution that grows with customers' ever-evolving, personal financial needs.
- Engage customers through the channels they are using in more and more facets of their life: mobile and voice.
- Grow engagement with the BofA mobile app.
- Increase customer satisfaction.
- Expand BofA's capabilities in machine learning and AI.

Solution

'One way we innovate is by engaging the entire organisation. We run innovation sessions throughout the year over a week or 24 hour period, we set a theme, we let teams self organise, they present to a panel of senior leadership to get feedback.'

Aditya Bhasin, Head of Consumer, Small Business, Wealth
Management and Employee Experience Technology Teams

Launched in 2018, Erica is the first widely available, AI-driven virtual financial assistant and dedicated personal financial tool in the US. Erica leverages the latest technology in AI, predictive

corporate finance advice, debt and equity market solutions, payments and cash management and trade and treasury services.

ING has a variety of ways of turning ideas into products and services. These include in-house innovations via ING Labs and partnering with fintechs and investing in fintechs via ING Ventures, the venture capital arm of ING. ING Ventures is a €300 million fund that targets disruptive technologies and helps entrepreneurs with hands-on support, know-how, scaling expertise and access to the bank's distribution network. ING has Labs in four cities around the world (Amsterdam, Brussels, London and Singapore), where the bank partners with others to bring disruptive ideas to market by combining its knowledge and network with their knowledge and skills. The bank has developed its own innovation framework called PACE, which is used to scale-up its most successful projects.

Problem

'We think of the world in terms of opportunities, not problems.'

Benoît Legrand, Chief Innovation Officer

Open banking and the introduction of EU's directive on payment services (PSD2) started shaking up the financial services world long before it became applicable in January 2018. Customer behaviour was changing at speed in response to new digital distribution channels, with expectations being framed by digital leaders in industries outside banking. It became clear that traditional banks would become endangered species unless they transformed themselves to meet customers' expectations.

In an increasingly competitive market, from non-banking players especially, the need to adapt to new user demands, technology and legislation was obvious for ING. The bank realised that experience, not products, would differentiate itself from the competition. Digital companies, like big tech and fintechs, were setting the experience benchmark, and they were setting it high. Customers expected the personalised and quick delivery services offered by companies such as Google, Netflix or Spotify to be mirrored by their banks. One thing was clear to ING: customers needed banking, not banks.

Solution

'There was no blueprint for how to set up a company within the bank, but the message to the team was always, "go do it", "don't compromise", "don't be afraid to disrupt ING".'

Frank Jan Risseeuw, Program Director

The vision was to focus on digital, platform-based business models, and be open to third parties. To turn that vision into reality, the bank started an internal transformation to become a dynamic digital financial services platform, at the heart of which was the belief that ING had to disrupt itself before someone else did. That meant a strategic focus on innovation to improve the customer experience and building and connecting to platforms that people used because they wanted to, not because they had no other choice.

ING's innovation culture includes a pragmatic open and collaborative approach, (1) where the bank has their own Labs to nurture potential fintechs (currently 25 initiatives in its innovation funnel), (2) where the bank invests through its venture capital arm, ING Ventures (currently more than 30 investments), and (3) where the bank partners with others outside of ING, like fintechs (currently more than 200 partnerships so far).

In order to explore the opportunities of open banking/PSD2 and ING's desire to disrupt itself, under ING's desire to disrupt itself, the bank launched Yolt into the UK market in 2017. Yolt is one of the first companies providing a platform for customers to manage money held by competitors, an example of ING's proactive approach towards open banking and platform thinking.

Before the project was approved by ING's management board on 13 October 2015, the bank's Strategy & Business Change team had done pre-project research to determine if there was a market for a multibank platform and, if so, what were the best markets to pilot such an initiative. This led the research team to the UK: a PSD2 country that hosted Yolt's target audience, millennials, tech-savvy young people who were not consciously managing their money, but who would benefit from doing so. The team originally focused on London given its similar size and demographic to other big cities in Europe and worldwide, which made it the perfect market for the team to test the app designed to become an international solution.

The Yolt team carried out a concept appetite test through qualitative research with focus groups in the UK. The results showed that a mobile app to connect all the financial products of users, making it possible for them to have a holistic view of their finances digitally, had great value and potential.

UK banking apps at the time did not mirror the technological developments available in the market. The apps tended to lack functionalities and were slow and difficult to navigate. While there were money management apps in the UK, their interfaces were not user friendly, and definitely not millennial friendly according to ING's research. Research showed that 25 to 34 year olds wanted 'snackable' insights in an appealing, visual feed. However, they also wanted money management apps to have the most basic functionalities that mobile banking apps had, such as transferring money, which was another functionality that money management apps in the UK were lacking.

In short, the team saw an opportunity to build an app that gave users a sense of control, made managing money easy, provided users with insight into their saving and spending behaviour and helped them keep up with a budget.

Solution

The approval of ING's management board marked the beginning of a 10-month research process. The Yolt team applied ING's PACE methodology to create a strong value proposition and validate their assumptions of what customers really wanted with experiments and customer feedback. PACE is a structured approach to innovation ING had set up to keep up with fintechs and other competitors that were transforming the financial industry.

First ING needed to understand customers' needs and the world they lived in, their pains and gains. The team focused on a number of themes such as millennials, managing money and creating habits.

Millennials were an interesting target group for Yolt because of their high adoption of digital banking, their general expectations when it came to digital solutions and their need to be increasingly careful with money (repaying student debt, buying their first home and working towards saving goals). These characteristics made them the ideal demographic for Yolt's launch. Whilst this original target audience was central to the app's initial development, the platform that has since been built enables Yolt to adapt the product to consumer attitudes at specific points in time, since the macroeconomic climate largely impacts these attitudes. They expect the easy, personalised services of tech giants and scale-up fintechs to be reflected by banks.

Their research found that everyone has the best intentions when it comes to managing their finances but many need to form a regular habit for this to become 'second nature' to the users. However, to create a habit, the bank needed to get to know their users very well.

By combining three studies on behavioural economics, the team created four types of users and defined a user engagement framework. The analysis showed that the focus should be on people who are not consciously managing their money, but who would benefit from doing so. The app would give users a clear, simple and easy way to have a more proactive approach towards managing their money.

This was applied at different parts of the app. For example, the transactional overview reflects the hunt for information, the ability to set and track budgets gives a sense of completion and the way of showing progress (on savings goals, for example) gives people the feeling of growing competence.

In parallel, the team carried out qualitative research in the Netherlands, consisting of desk research, expert interviews and focus groups. Based on the input from the focus groups, the team created six hypotheses, which were tested on a larger scale in the UK. A thousand people were asked by ING Group Research about their experiences and view on money management.

Since ING did not have a retail presence in the UK, the bank teamed up with an expert agency on app development. Together,

colleagues in the UK. In October 2016, the team released a closed beta version of the app, also known as Private Beta, to a restricted group of 2,500 users in the market. That also marked the moment when the team could talk about Yolt in the press.

In June 2017, the product became available in Open Beta. Within six months, the team celebrated 100,000 app downloads.

Since the PSD2 regulation launched in January 2018, Yolt had worked with the Open Banking Implementation Entity to set up application programming interfaces (APIs), allowing it to access financial information from other banks. That same month, Yolt became the first third-party provider to complete a successful connection with an incumbent bank under the new (at the time) open banking system.

Yolt dashboard

Results

Yolt's launch in 2017 marked ING's return to the UK market. The app was made available to only 2,500 customers while it remained in beta testing. ING got ahead of the game by launching Yolt, preparing itself for the open banking regulation that was introduced a year later.

At the beginning, the focus was on growth but also largely centred around building trust with users. Many consumers were being scorned by increases in cybercrime and therefore nervous to use a new app to manage their sensitive financial matters. To this day, Yolt is very much focused not only on the product offering with the app but also on the educational content it produces to educate both consumers and businesses on the benefits of open banking technology.

ING's KPIs for Yolt were growth, registered users, monthly active users, as well as customer satisfaction measured via ratings and reviews. Within six months from the launch, the app registered 100,000 downloads. The Yolt team closely monitored the reviews from the app store, social media, closed communities or received by email.

Key Learnings

Their biggest learning was the importance of that initial beta period where they really put the user in the driving seat. This approach allowed them to re-inform the product based on real, tangible feedback from their target audience, who were real people with real life financial goals. This, in turn, meant that when the product did launch publicly, they already had a strong community of early adopters engaging with the Yolt app.

Another observation was the importance of local research and adopting the go-to-market strategy before launching in new markets. Cultural differences are at play, even when launching the exact same product in multiple markets. For example, Italy is more cash-driven and hence having a view of their transactions is not as important for Italian consumers, with most transactions done manually. Likewise, the levels of trust in banking services and the availability of other competitors' services vastly differ per market, and these have an impact on the sentiment towards their product. Another important aspect was the difference in the digital adoption of open banking services across markets, which also differed vastly between the UK, Italy and France.

The availability and stability of APIs across markets under PSD2 took longer to become available than they would have hoped.

What's Next

Since the Yolt app launched three years ago, over 1.6 million registered users have downloaded the app and the team have continued to listen to users and develop the app further. In October 2020, Yolt launched a series of innovative features to help users to save. The new features, rooted in behavioural science, enable people to form saving habits through small tweaks to their daily routines and easy automatic actions within the app. The new features include an option to round up purchases to the pound, for example, and automatically put the 'extra' money into a 'money jar'.

The new money jar feature also offers handy tips and reminders for users to increase their savings. It is trained to recognise and save refunds, salary raises and even bonuses.

Users can switch on automatic options like 'the cashback collector' and earn cashback rewards with their favourite retailers or activate 'the set saver' to automatically move money from their Yolt account to the money jar either daily, weekly or monthly.

Chapter 10
Santander
Building In-house, Spinning Out

Case: Sim

Executive Summary

Santander is one of the largest banks in Europe and has extended operations across North and South America, and more recently in continental Asia. This case originates from Santander Brasil.

Despite Brazil having one of the most promising economies among emerging countries and a population of more than 200 million people it has an unbanked population of more than 45 million, along with millions of informal entrepreneurs who face difficulties in accessing credit lines suitable to their needs.

In 2019 Santander Brasil launched Sim, a fintech focused on digital loans to individuals. It was launched after six months of work and is, after one year, one of the largest fintechs in this segment.

In its first year of operation, more than three million customers simulated with Sim, over R$800 million were lent, their NPS (Net Promoter Score) reached 80 and the business has been profitable from the outset.

Introductions

Do you want more details about this case? Find additional highlights from these interviews at www.howbanksinnovate.com.

Geraldo Rodrigues, Director of Digital Business, Santander Brasil

Geraldo has dedicated 20 years to the financial industry, 18 of them to Banco Santander. In this long trajectory, he was responsible for the Santander Insurance operation in both Brazil and Mexico. He also had a brief passage at the Bank's Retail operation in the interior of São Paulo. He is currently Director of Digital Business for Santander Brasil and responsible for two New Ventures of the Group (Sim and emDia).

Vinicius Aloe, CEO, Sim

Vini has been with Santander since 2009 and has been leading Sim since 2019. He has worked in the industry for 15 years, across Credit, Pricing, Risk Management, Analytics and Retail positions. Vini holds a Master's Degree in Risk Management from Insper and a Bachelor's Degree in Business Administration from the University of Sao Paulo.

Gabriel Minchilo, Business Development Manager, Sim

Gabriel started at Santander in 2016 as a trainee. After three years working with product and business development at Santander he joined Sim in 2019. Gabriel holds a Bachelor's Degree in Production Engineering, a Green Belt certificate and has international experience at Clemson University.

Background

Key Figures

Total assets: €1.5 trillion
Number of customers: 145 million
Number of branches: 12,000
Number of full-time employees: 200,000
(Approximate as of 2020)

Santander is one of the largest banks in Europe and has extended operations across North and South America, and more recently in continental Asia. This case originates from Santander in Brasil so we will focus on their background specifically.

Santander Brasil is the third largest private bank in the country. Its stores, 'PABs' (Banking Service Points), ATMs, regional offices, technology hubs and culture centres can be found in all regions of Brazil.

The operations of Santander Brazil have two major business units: commercial banking, which combines its retail activities, such as service to individuals and small- and medium-sized enterprises; and wholesale, dedicated to serving large companies and the capital market.

Santander's Brazilian unit, headquartered in São Paulo, has been operating since 1982 and acts as an autonomous subsidiary in terms of capital and liquidity, adapting itself to operational and regulatory characteristics. This is the case in all the markets where Santander is present, in an arrangement that segregates risks between its different business units.

The operations of Santander Brasil are inspired by the global purpose of helping people and businesses prosper, acting in a simple, personal and fair way. This guides the culture, decision-making and behaviour of Santander in Brazil, as well as the companies in its ecosystem.

Problem

Despite having one of the most promising economies among emerging countries and a population of more than 200 million people it has an unbanked population of more than 45 million, along with millions of informal entrepreneurs who face difficulties in accessing credit lines suitable to their needs. The sheer size of the country makes it difficult for banks to offer a consistency of services across the region.

This scenario means that nearly 65% of personal loan transactions in Brazil are concentrated in the five largest banks, unlike more mature markets, such as the United States and Europe. On the one hand, banks are doing a good job extending credit to existing customers, since they will have highly valuable transaction history data to support the credit assessment. However, having to first become a customer and generate a sufficient amount of historical data to be considered for credit, acts as an entry barrier for a lot of new customers. While the vast majority of traditional financial companies also lend to consumers with a riskier credit profile, they have limited digital offering, unattractive rates and low approval rates. The offer of personal loans with competitive terms and a seamless lending journey for customers who are not account holders ends up being strikingly limited.

Another aspect that is particular to the Brazilian market is its high interest and non-performing loan rates. This is a vicious cycle that is difficult to break and requires better risk assessments so customers are presented with better offers. In this context, vehicle-backed loans are not widely used in Brazil, despite the country's fleet of over 30 million fully paid vehicles that could be used as collateral by customers.

As such, access to credit at competitive rates fails to reach the entire population in the same way. This backdrop suggested a demand that was being poorly met: to serve a large portion of the population in a digital and scalable manner, providing customers with credit on fair terms.

Amid this landscape, over 600 fintechs emerged in Brazil between 2016 and 2019, many of them with the aim of granting loans digitally, despite the fact that this is an extremely complex activity that requires highly specific expertise in risk management, funding and technology, as it takes place in an environment with non-performing loan and potential fraud rates among the highest in the world. That being the case, the combination of all fintech companies in the market very likely would not achieve a total share of 1% in 2018.

The most successful examples of disruptors in this space were found abroad. Most of them were companies that showed the ability to combine the scale, know-how and expertise of large banks and financial institutions with the agility, nimbleness, efficiency and customer-centric experience of fintechs.

Faced with these problems, Santander Brasil realised that there was an opportunity to serve an audience that demanded new services and products: consumers with little access to or interest in credit conditions available from banks to account holders or traditional financial companies. There was room to create a digital loan solution focused on the open market.

From a business model and project perspective, there was also another problem to be addressed. How should Santander approach this project? Should they buy a promising fintech already operating on this market? Could they develop something from within their own departments and a core project management model? Should they try to build it from scratch as an independent company? There is not only one right approach but the team knew that for this venture to be successful they would need to achieve their best while being part of a large and solid group but, at the same time, to enjoy the speed and shorter deliver–learn–react cycle seen in smaller and more agile companies.

Solution

'We have created a Hub of New Business, where employees can sub-mit ideas. If an idea is taken forward, the hub incubates them until they are ready to be spun-out into their own businesses – that is how Sim started its journey.'

Geraldo Rodrigues, Director of Digital Business,
Santander Brasil

In 2019 Santander Brasil launched Sim, a fintech focused on digital loans to individuals. It was launched after six months of work and is, after one year, one of the largest tech companies in this sector operating on the open market in Brazil.

The business opportunity was clear: the objective was to democratise access to credit with a low entry barrier, competitive conditions for customers and sustainable results. The path, how-ever, was not as clear. Whilst Santander have a range of existing tech solutions in terms of products across different markets, there was still doubt as to which would be the best model for this new business catering to the open digital market: building an in-house solution, acquiring a company that already had the solution or finding a partner to complement the services. The wrong choice could have a high cost, after all, as time-to-market and reaction ability were crucial, since several players were also moving quickly to capture this opportunity.

After evaluating the alternatives, Santander Brasil decided to build a new solution from scratch. The strategy was to develop a hybrid model, combining the best of the 'traditional' banking world with the speed and flexibility of an independent fintech, a model that had already proven itself in other markets. If they were suc-cessful, it meant that they would also be creating a benchmark and learning opportunity for the bank in the future.

The first obstacle had been overcome, but with the decision made, other questions began to arise. Who should own this initiative? Which technological architecture to use? What products to sell?

In January 2019, following a few weeks of debate, Vinicius Aloe, current CEO of Sim and until then Head of People Analytics at Santander, with experience in Credit, Pricing, Risk and Retail positions, accepted the challenge of building a multiproduct 'credit as a service' platform targeting the open market from the ground up. This new company would have to be secure and highly scalable, and it would also have to be put into operation quickly so that, in the midst of building a strong business, it could learn in practice how to react to customer demands in a timely manner. The go-to-market period proposed to the Santander Group was only six months.

The first month of the so-called 'Red project' was entirely devoted to laying out a blueprint for what the company was going to be. After numerous conversations with several business leaders, market benchmarks and sleepless nights dedicated to understanding competitors, setting up the business plan, prototyping and testing with customers, the first design of what would be built in the coming months materialised.

Developing a platform from square one within a timeframe of just six months involves difficult choices, not only to identify what needs to be done, but especially to determine what not to do. The focus on choosing what would really bring value to customers and sustainability to the business is part of the essence that has been in place since the dawn of the new company. To put the plan into action, the first two key challenges were clear: building a diverse and high-performance team of specialists and creating a truly robust and scalable credit, product and technology architecture.

Over the first few months, a great deal of energy was spent on selecting and forming a diverse, specialist team, with a high degree of training and technical professionalism that would operate in an agile work structure. More than half of the initial team would be dedicated to technology, credit and analytics, while the rest would be tasked with attracting customers, digital marketing, products and customer happiness. Important support functions that are not core business areas (such as Human Resources and Legal, for example) operated in a synergistic 'as a service' model in collaboration with Santander from the outset. The team was looking for individuals with an entrepreneurial spirit, autonomy and the ability to fit culturally into a reality of intense learning, constant changes and quick reaction.

One of the greatest challenges of an open market platform is to stabilise credit and fraud control from a digital acquisition channel with a low entry barrier. To overcome this adversity, the team focused on building the best-in-class credit architecture with the purpose of prevailing over the solutions available on the market. Hinged on the expertise of the bank's different businesses and on the most advanced engines, bureaus and queries, policies and fraud control mechanisms, it became possible to build a legacy-free architecture that concatenated the best of the already established companies with a completely new technology filled with additional features. The objective was to quickly conceive and deploy an extraordinarily powerful platform for fraud and credit control.

During the months that followed, the plan was implemented after a number of route corrections along the way, resulting from unforeseen events and lessons learned from execution. To decide what not to do proved to be even more important in this environment because the team had tight deadlines and there were high expectations on quality. Getting the execution right was paramount during this phase of the project in particular. To build a culture that really understands and focus on what matters and at the same time that operates well in a hybrid model (large company sometimes, startup sometimes) was one of the greatest challenges. Cultural fit besides technical excellence was a major concern in every hire and partnership decision. In this embryonic company, activities ranged from the definition of colours, brand and tone of voice to the signing of contracts with suppliers, the approval of global committees and the creation of fully online collateral assessment systems.

Six months later, in the spring of 2019, more specifically on 23 September, Empréstimo Sim was born, a digital platform aimed at transforming and democratising the credit market. In just a few seconds, any non-account holder would be able to access Sim and visualise a credit offer for their profile, either without collateral, or by using their car or motorcycle as collateral to borrow at more advantageous rates. Everything could be done digitally, on a mobile phone.

Delivery

'We wanted to create an open market solution that could scale without a lot of cost; we realised it would be much easier to do that if it was built from scratch, leveraging the know-how from the bank when it suited us'.

Vinicius Aloe, CEO, Sim

One year after the launch, processes and journeys were introduced and others removed. Products were launched and later discontinued. Important people came and left. Some goals have been exceeded, others have been revised and some have not been achieved. All this while surrounded by unexpected economic, social and personal circumstances. Countless hypotheses had been discussed, tested, discarded or enhanced, and with all this learning, the result has also come to light.

Since its first customer, a self-employed person from the State of Sergipe who needed financial assistance for his small grocery store, Sim has become one of the more high-profile credit startups on the Brazilian market. It is a multiproduct (personal loans, car equity, consumer finance, credit card, insurance) marketplace platform with a credit and fraud architecture designed and tested in the digital open market, profitable from its first year.

The team has been through the 'the project' phase, in which the ambition to launch a robust and efficient, but flexible, solution in a particularly short period of time has passed. The goal back then was to quickly learn from customers and adapt to what was found.

The time to prove itself 'as a product', whose priority was to find a basic formula to attract and generate value for customers with a solid profitability hypothesis, has also gone by. Those were the months in which the daily lives of the teams were consumed by quickly building, correcting and calibrating offers, journeys, architecture, products, services, channels, policies, scripts and squads. All this was often done with little validated information and tight deadlines.

Sim has today reached the stage of being an actual company, in its own right. With more scale, they have witnessed the first results and received feedback on what had already been built. On the one hand, Sim has become more scientific, organised and data driven. On the other hand, mistakes and blind spots have far greater consequences (and opportunities). The focus on building remains enormous, but other responsibilities, such as control, stability, adjustment of expectations and route correction, have gained the same relevance. Now more than ever, the opportunity cost is huge and choosing where to invest time and resources is the biggest challenge.

Results

With a strategy focused on gaining scale in a profitable way, Sim has built a flexible acquisition model (B2C and B2B2C) that currently has more than 15 partners distributing products and services on their own platforms.

In its first year of operation, more than three million customers simulated with Sim, over R$800 million were lent, their NPS (Net Promoter Score) reached 80 and the business has been profitable from the outset.

Sim is an example of 'bantech' in the Santander ecosystem and in the industry: extracting the best from 'being tech', with little legacy, new technology, squad oriented, nimbleness, full integration and focus, and combining it with the best from 'being a bank', with consolidated expertise, highly specialized human capital, scale, soundness, core banking solutions and funding.

Learnings

'The hardest thing was to prioritise what features we were launching with, it is hard to choose what not to do, because we wanted to do it all. Knowing what I know today, I wish we had started the customer testing much earlier.'

Gabriel Minchilo, Business Development Manager, Sim

There is clearly not one right approach to deliver innovation. The bank can build in-house, using the existing tools and people. The bank can acquire or invest in other businesses in the space they wish to move into.

The team at Sim feel that the bank would not have been as successful had they not agreed to build this from scratch, outside the regular structures. From the complexity of orchestrating different departments and agendas, the relevant IT and product legacy and the bias of repeating established business models would have hurt the speed and ability to brainstorm execute–learn–react really fast.

Another key takeaway is the importance of getting the execution right. Building a culture that talks about what not to do is as important as understanding what can be done better.

What's Next

Santander knows that the only way Sim will continue to grow is to excel at understanding and delivering the best solutions. Key to this is to continue to innovate. The bank will continue to evaluate what new opportunities to pursue by building, buying or partnering.

Despite having achieved encouraging results in its first year of operation, this is just the beginning for Sim. The ambition is to transform the credit market at an annual pace of 1% and deliver even more significant results to Santander.

Part III
Partner

Chapter 11
Deutsche Bank
Partnering with fintechs

Case: Deposit Solutions

Executive Summary

To realise Deutsche Bank's (DB) digitalisation strategy, partnering with fintechs was identified as essential, offering more agility, innovation and an increased speed to market. This was demonstrated by the launch of ZinsMarkt, DB's digital marketplace offering for fixed-term deposits from multiple banks. Building on a white label platform provided by a fintech called Deposit Solutions, DB managed to launch a new digital proposition that gave its customers access to products from other banks while DB retained the customer ownership.

ZinsMarkt has had to overcome numerous challenges: a lack of marketing activities, missing management commitment, no sales focus and a small number of offers in early stages of the project. The final breakthrough happened in 2020, three years after go live, by developing a multichannel access to the platform, incentivising the sales advisors and providing a dedicated budget.

Until now, over €4.5 billion in deposits of retail customers have been placed with the ZinsMarkt partner banks and there are multiple opportunities to scale the platform further in terms of target customers, features, partner banks as well as markets.

Introductions

Do you want more details about this case? Find additional highlights from these interviews at www.howbanksinnovate.com.

Christoph Zschätzsch, Head of Investment Products, Insurances and Deposits

Christoph is responsible for managing the full range of investment products and related processes across the two brands Deutsche Bank and Postbank, such as online broker maxblue and robo advisor Robin. He also looks after the insurance partnerships with Zurich and Talanx as well as Deutsche Bank's retail deposit products, such as ZinsMarkt. Prior to his current role, Christoph was heading the Mortgage and Consumer Finance Business for Private & Business Clients. Over his career at the bank Christoph has gained deep insights into overall bank steering and strategy processes and a deep understanding of retail banking products, processes and overall management. Christoph studied Business Management at the Johannes Gutenberg University of Mainz and the Paris Nanterre University.

Thorsten Rexhausen, Director, ZinsMarkt

Thorsten has been working for Deutsche Bank since 1991. After his apprenticeship, he has held a number of positions and started doing in-house consulting on various IT projects such as implementing SAP. In the meantime, he redefined the operating model of the mid and back offices across Europe. Since 2016, he has been contributing to the digitalization of the bank. In this role, he developed, launched, and is in charge of the deposit marketplace ZinsMarkt.

Dr Tim Sievers, CEO and Founder, Deposit Solutions

Tim started Deposit Solutions in 2011 and is a pioneer in the fintech industry. He is an active contributor to the community, as a member of the Fintech Committee of the Federal Ministry of Finance, the Digital Banking Project Committee of the Association of German Banks and as a speaker at conferences. Prior to Deposit Solutions, Tim worked for 10 years in private equity and technology companies. He holds a doctorate in Economics from the University of Hamburg, an MSc in Economics from the London School of Economics and Political Science and an MA in Politics, Philosophy and Economics from the University of Oxford.

Background

Key Figures

Total assets: €1.3 trillion
Number of customers: 22 million
Number of branches: 2,000
Number of full-time employees: 90,000
(Approximate as of 2020)

Deutsche Bank (DB) was founded in 1870 and is the largest bank in Germany with operations across Europe and a significant presence in the Asia Pacific region and the Americas. The company is one of the largest foreign exchange dealers in the world. They provide retail and private banking, corporate and transaction banking, lending, asset and wealth management products and services, as well as focused investment banking to private individuals, small- and medium-sized companies, corporations, governments and institutional investors.

The bank started its current transformation journey in 2018. In the first phase they stabilised the bank, for example by reducing risks and bolstering their capital position. In 2019 they started phase two, the most fundamental transformation of the bank in two decades. This transformation includes a new strategy and a new setup for the bank: they exited non-strategic businesses and assets and focused on market-leading businesses. By 2020, the bulk of the transformation and restructuring work was completed. Having re-focused their business model, they are now in the third and final phase of their transformation. Their focus now is on ensuring sustainable profitability by growing their businesses while remaining disciplined on costs and capital.

Problem

Like in many markets, the banking environment in Germany is challenging and is affected by political, economic and legal changes, e.g. the increased regulations in response to the last financial crisis. In addition, the expansionary monetary policy of the European Central Bank makes it difficult for banks to offer attractive returns, for instance on fixed-term deposits, and simultaneously this leads to profitability pressure in the private clients business.

Meanwhile, a technical and sociocultural factor has been revolutionising the banking industry with regards to digitalisation. It is the biggest game-changer in the banking industry for decades. The relevance of the digital revolution does not only come from the technology deployed, but also from the change in customer behaviour and the increase in customer expectations. Instead of meeting the advisor at a branch, customers are increasingly using digital access channels to handle their daily banking needs. Transparency of banking products has greatly increased through the Internet but also by regulations. Customers can easily access information and are able to compare prices and services. As basic banking products are mostly simple, interchangeable and often differ only by the price, switching costs for customers are relatively low. If customers do not get what they expect they are simply switching banks. Hence, with progressive digitalisation, new behavioural patterns arise, which will fundamentally change the interaction between banks and their customers. In addition, with digitalisation, new competitors like fintech and big tech are entering the market, offering innovative technical solutions for the financial sector and thus posing a threat of substitute products as they are trying to gain market share from traditional banks.

As a result, DB faced the problem of increased competition, declining margins and not being able to offer their clients reasonable interest rates caused by the overall low interest environment. DB's Chief Digital Officer quickly realised that it does not make sense to fight those new competitors, but rather ally with them to make use of their benefits, such as agility and innovation. Fortunately, this was around the time that Dr Tim Sievers, CEO of Deposit Solutions, approached DB introducing their fintech and white label open banking solution. The platform did not present a solution for an existing problem as such, but presented a brand new opportunity the bank had not considered in the past. It would allow DB to offer third-party products while maintaining the customer relationship and generating a new source of revenue.

DB felt that if it did not partner with Deposit Solutions, other banks could and probably would, and that meant DB could lose potential new business and customers. If you cannot beat them, join them.

Before deciding to enter into the partnership with Deposit Solutions, DB looked at building a similar platform in-house. Whilst there was a central budget they could use, there was not enough IT resources available to deliver the project in a reasonable period of time. They also realised that by not using the budget, they could save that towards other projects where a partnership was not on offer. Based on internal estimates, the time to market was almost half when launching this in partnership with a fintech, compared to building this in-house. As such, the decision was made to enter into cooperation with Deposit Solutions and use their white label solution as the basis for the platform and benefit from the time, money and effort already invested in their existing platform. In addition, DB was also able to benefit from the first mover advantage, as no other major bank was offering anything like this at the time.

At this time DB did not have a team responsible for sourcing, evaluating and partnering with fintechs and had no real experience with innovation management. This resulted in a lot of people doing the same thing, taking the same meetings multiple times, creating a lot of unnecessary work internally as well as for the potential fintech partners.

As the number of different digital initiatives grew, as well as the need to manage them more effectively, DB set up the 'Digital Office' who centrally managed innovation with the help of an innovation funnel approach. Their main function was to manage the budgets, track all projects, evaluate success, etc. The budgets were allocated on a quarterly basis, which made it difficult and time consuming for the business units to ask for money over and over again. As the larger projects would run for more than a quarter, this risk of start/stop in case additional funds had not been allocated in a timely manner was also counterproductive.

Solution

'Partnering with a fintech makes a lot of sense in areas that are complimentary to your core competencies.'

Christoph Zschätzsch, Head of Investment Products,
Insurances and Deposits

The rise of digital innovators in financial services presents a significant threat to the business models of traditional banks. Customer expectations are evolving and require banks to understand and respond to needs. Customers tend to move quicker towards the best offerings. As a result, Deutsche Bank did not want to offer only their own customer savings products and selected Deposit Solutions to operate the bank's exclusive retail deposit marketplace, which was still the first of its kind for a major bank. Deposit Solutions operates a platform that connects banks in search of retail funding with other institutions that have a customer base interested in saving, allowing banks to collect deposits from people across Europe who are not necessarily their direct customers. Any bank can easily connect to Deposit Solutions' open banking platform through APIs. In several product categories, such as mutual funds, mortgage loans or structured products, adding third-party products has already been a common practice for banks for decades. This logic is now also applied to the deposit business.

The open banking platform changes the rules for all participants. Building upon Deposit Solutions' white label solution of open banking technology, Deutsche Bank launched 'ZinsMarkt' in 2017 and established themselves as a central financial point of sale for their customers by offering fixed-term deposits from other European banks that pay higher interest. The onboarding of third-party banks to the platform is standardised. It allows product banks to source deposit funding on to their home balance sheet without having to take care of customer acquisitions, account management, customer service, etc. They increase the size of their addressable market and benefit from exact controllability of volumes and maturities. On the other hand, customers gain access to a large range of products from numerous banks in different countries via a single source. The marketplace is fully integrated into Deutsche Bank's online banking, allowing customers to access it anytime, anywhere. Additionally, ZinsMarkt is offered as a service through client advisors at the bank's branches. Deutsche Bank customers can easily build up a portfolio of deposit products through their DB home account. The digital end-to-end new customer process enabled customers to deposit money in less than 10 minutes and simultaneously open a ZinsMarkt personal account, which also relieves the back-office units.

Deutsche Bank sees digitalisation as one key lever to optimise its cost position, in order to improve efficiency and on the other side to invent new business models. To realise this digitalisation strategy, fintechs as Deposit Solution are essential as partners, offering higher agility and faster time-to-market. In times of strong competition, it is crucial to be fast in implementing innovations.

DB has started to move toward agile ways of working to speed up the delivery of new products and services. However, no digital transformation comes without problems. Deutsche Bank has a large and complex organisational structure with legacy regulatory, technological and cultural restrictions. Process dependencies and silo mentality created unnecessary friction. To make progress it became apparent that they had to install a culture of agility and collaboration throughout all involved departments, which included regular communication. Many discussions were needed to convince the decision-makers of the advantages of this new sales opportunity as the main fear was that any innovation could cannibalise their existing products.

In 2016 the bank created a specialised department called the Chief Digital Office and set aside a €750 million budget for digital products and services until 2020. This department focused on the development of strategic initiatives within the scope of the digital agenda. Within the Chief Digital Office, there was one team in charge of the digital roadmap as well as the budget. For a new project to be funded, it had to add commercial value and profit and have a business case to back it up. Exceptions were made for innovations that enabled other strategic objectives to be achieved.

Another challenge the bank had to overcome was to align new product and service delivery with the sales and marketing channels. They were of course required to raise awareness about each project, not just for customers, but also internally. Previously the sales and marketing departments were executing their own agenda and had little visibility or awareness of what was coming down the pipeline.

Delivery

'Banks have multiple challenges; legacy systems, regulation, operating at scale and so on, so in many ways it is natural for banks to experiment with innovation by partnering with a fintech instead.'

Dr Tim Sievers, CEO and Founder, Deposit Solutions

When Deposit Solutions approached DB in 2015, the request was handed over to the product management for analysis and the project was set up with only very little dedicated resources. Only one person on the business side was allocated to this project, as the project did not have a high management priority at the start. As the main reason for partnering with a fintech was to do things quickly, this lack of commitment made no sense as it slows everything down and the intended benefits could not be realised. With a management change in 2016, the project was re-staffed and kicked-off for good. A team of three existing employees as well as three external consultants were dedicated to this project in August 2016, with the goal to go live nine months later, in May 2017. Tight project plans were created and colleagues from IT, online banking, communications, marketing and sales were involved to ensure a timely go live. Due to this size of the team working very closely, those involved said it felt like working in a small startup within the bank, with flat hierarchy, a lot of own responsibilities and a steep learning curve. All project members were completely committed to the project and believed in the idea as a new revenue stream for the bank while adding value for the customers at the same time. Only through this high dedication was the team able to stick to the project plan and to go live in time.

The original idea and scope were downsized to meet the go live target date. The team decided for a phased roll-out, starting with an MVP approach: building a digital platform including a pure online contract creation process, only to a small group of customers, and also only one partner bank to start with. The group of customers that would be eligible for this was those of maxblue, the online broker of Deutsche Bank Private Bank. Whilst those customers are using maxblue to invest, and this was about savings, they were still chosen as they are digitally savvy and used to self-service to take the pressure off DB to educate new users.

For the ZinsMarkt go live a holistic launch management concept was developed, including classic communication measures like Intranet news, FAQs, roadshows and internal WebEx sessions. At this time, there were also initiatives to familiarise the organisation with digitalisation overall, which was also leveraged by the ZinsMarkt team. Besides the internal measures, there was no external communication at all. Looking back, the team can say that it was not really an 'MVP' approach from the agile theory. The scope was indeed downsized but it still had a lot of functionalities that would not have been necessary in the beginning.

After going live, the team had a hard time to establish ZinsMarkt as a brand within the bank as well as externally. It was built as a purely digital product; thus, there was no sales focus and sales people were not interested as they had a lot of topics and various other products on their desks. Moreover, there was no external marketing (budget) at all since there was only one partner bank onboarded, so one could not yet talk about this being a true market place. Because of this, nobody knew about this platform and the number of customers and volumes were extremely low. The internal team persisted and promoted the platform throughout the bank trying to get more people familiar with it. Only in May 2018 with the onboarding of a second bank as well as inviting the wider DB customer base to use it and external press releases did marketing start.

The real breakthrough happened in 2020 when the bank decided to bring ZinsMarkt to the branches and build a dedicated ZinsMarkt frontend for the customer advisors. The most important lever was to incentivise the sales advisors and the increase in volume was significant. As it is a two-sided marketplace the challenge is still to balance offerings and demand at the same time. This is quite tough currently, as the demand continuously increases, while it is challenging to onboard new partner banks, as they have to meet the requirements of DB, e.g. deposit protection and security.

In terms of project management and development, over the duration of this project the team switched to agile working methods and, as a result, they now do monthly releases, bringing innovation and process improvements faster to the customers.

Results

'This partnership became a catalyst for us to shift from waterfall to agile and today over 80% of our projects are agile.'

Thorsten Rexhausen, Director, ZinsMarkt

The data shows that economic uncertainties as well as internal sales incentive measures simultaneously have a strong impact on the success of the platform. In general, new offers with particularly good interest rates lead to an increase in volumes. As a result, over €4.5 billion in deposits of retail customers have been placed with the ZinsMarkt partner banks as of 2020.

The initial lack of marketing activities and a small number of offers meant that the volume of deposits grew very slowly at the start. It was only after the launch of additional banks, the addition of more offers and marketing activities that triggered a sudden and sustained increase, tripling the deposits initially, and after four months even increased sixfold. From 2018 to 2019, the volume of deposits rose by roughly 200%.

This result is now to be multiplied continuously by expanding customer segments and extending offerings and features. A high potential lies in the expansion of the platform for corporate customers, which in return also requires an additional number of dedicated offerings. Further opportunities with regard to the bank's international activities are given by an expansion to foreign countries with a strong deposit demand or to include specific offerings with different currencies.

Results are not just measured in numbers. What was started as a project to help customers became a catalyst for the bank to develop its capabilities to enter into more partnerships and execute them more effectively going forward. Thanks to the partnership with

Deposit Solutions, using their white label technology, DB managed to launch a new digital proposition that gave its customers access to products from other banks while DB retained the customer ownership and opened up a new revenue stream. Whilst ZinsMarkt has grown significantly in the past year, it has still only scratched the surface and has a lot more room to grow in the coming years. In Germany alone, the volume of savings deposits amounts to €2.5 trillion every year.

On the back of the success with ZinsMarkt, DB has since taken a 4.9% equity stake in Deposit Solutions, which is now a fintech unicorn. DB's investment is the first time Deposit Solutions has allowed one of its clients to become a co-owner.

Learnings

It is essential to invest in new business models in order to tap into new revenue pools and secure long-term success.

From the bank's perspective, a key takeaway is focus. It would have been easier to achieve the desired results when you focus on a small number of projects and would also have helped senior management stay engaged and focused. This also links back to assurances around funding. Budgets should have been ring-fenced for each project and been set for a fixed period of time. Certainty around funding would have decreased the external influences through constant budget-cut discussions and would ensure greater planning certainty, which would have increased the speed to market and learnings to be acted on.

With regards to partnering with fintechs, the key to success is to agree what a true MVP should look like, e.g. one product, one target customer group. Getting a basic MVP to be stable is critical before thinking about scaling it. Banks should not consider every possible use case, so they too have to hold back and stay focused.

Above all, it is critical to get sales, marketing and communications onboard and aligned, for without a plan and incentives, no partnership will succeed.

What's Next

Adopting new technologies continues to be a critical part of DB's strategy. Many areas of the bank are on the lookout for digital solutions to meet their individual challenges and often rely on the ideas of tech companies to do so.

Finding suitable providers and integrating their technologies in the bank is an on-going challenge. That is where the global presence of DB's Innovation Network offices comes in, based in Berlin, London, New York, Palo Alto, as well as Singapore covering the Asia Pacific region. The bank's Innovation Network members continuously scout, identify and evaluate the solutions provided by startups and technology companies and marry them with the requirements of the business divisions and/or control and infrastructure functions.

It follows a demand-driven model. It usually starts with a specific question from an internal business function owner, employees or clients. The Innovation Labs facilitate the entire process of technology adoption, from the problem definition up to selection of the vendor. The final phase is the signing of a production commercial agreement and the implementation of the solution by the respective department.

In Santa Ana, California, DB's Document Custody Service team verifies loan documents for clients such as real estate, auto or solar loan documents, before they can be funded, securitised or sold. To accelerate the highly manual process with several truckloads of documents being handled each day, they applied an artificial intelligence solution from a New York based startup working in combination with high-speed scanners. Today over 20,000 loans are being processed each day involving scanning and analysing of around half a million pages a day.

Chapter 12
Danske Bank
Partnering with startups

Case: +Impact, TheHub, Danske Bank Growth

Executive Summary

Danske Bank (DB) formed the Growth & Impact initiative in late 2015, based on the trends that the startups of today will be the big companies of tomorrow and that they will be based on tech and have sustainability at their core or as an important element of the way they operate. At the same time, the bank also recognised the need to re-invent banking in order to be able to cater for that segment.

That led to a way of working with partners from the ecosystem, an agile setup with very tight relations to the customer segment. This has resulted in the development and launch of a suite of both commercial and non-commercial offerings, of which one of them is the digital platform +impact.

The +impact platform is one of the non-commercial activities. It targets impact startups, a subsegment of startups that have sustainability at the core of their business and the potential to scale.

The platform was created in collaboration with a third-party partner with a stronghold with the segment, and illustrates how the Growth & Impact team in Danske Bank seek to work as a startup in order to be relevant to the segment.

They stress their learning of having the right mandate, using strong partners, being an integrated part of the eco-system and the importance of constant user validation as the key to succeed.

Introductions

Do you want more details about this case? Find additional highlights from these interviews at www.howbanksinnovate.com.

Klavs Hjort, SVP and Head of Growth & Impact

Klavs is responsible for DB's activities in the Nordics towards startups and impact startups. He was the founder and lead behind the Danske Bank Growth & Impact initiative, with a focus on creating solutions for startups across the Nordics that want to scale their business and impact. Klavs has a background in DB as SVP of Business Innovation and Sales & Customer Engagement. His educational background is from IMD and Copenhagen Business School.

Leadership Team. The Head of Business Banking had been involved in this process since an early stage, together with the Head of Business Development in Business Banking. Having spotted the issue and raised the importance of this opportunity, SVP Klavs Hjort became the main lead of the initiative.

In the beginning, the bank used a typical approach for business development using internal resources paired with Tier 1 management consultants. It soon became clear that the process did not give the insights and results required, and it also became apparent that the bank and advisors did not have the mindset needed to find the right solutions for the startup and scaleup segment.

Instead, the bank turned to the venture building company, Rainmaking. Rainmaking was founded by a small group of entrepreneurs, had a strong foothold in the global startup ecosystem and demonstrated an ability to launch and grow new platforms and services at high speed.

In a very short time, the digital platform the Hub (thehub.io) was launched. The Hub addressed one of the startups' most pressing challenges, namely that of recruiting talent and finding funding and best practice tools.

Since the launch in late 2015, the Hub has developed into the largest market place for startup jobs and talent in the Nordics. Today it includes more than 8,000 startup profiles, 28,000 jobs have been posted since the start, which again have had more than 500,000 applicants. In addition, it has worked to create more transparency between startups and investors in the funding process, with more than 1,000 investor profiles. On a daily basis, the Hub is run by Rainmaking.

This way of working, with partners from the ecosystem, an agile setup and very tight relations to the customer segment, has led to the development and launch of a suite of offerings within the Growth & Impact area of the bank. The offerings are both commercial and non-commercial, and are all focused on helping startups and scaleups grow their business and impact. The initiatives target various steps in the lifecycle of a startup, from early stage over growth to consolidation.

One of the initiatives that has spun off from this approach is the +impact initiative, which is one of the non-commercial activities, initiated in December 2017. The initiative taps into the sustainability trend and target impact startups, which is the subsegment of startups and scaleups that addresses one or more of the UN Sustainable Development Goals at the core of their business and have potential to scale.

The first step of the +impact initiative was to create an in-depth understanding of the impact startups and identify the problems that prevented this subsegment from scaling their business. An analysis showed that the impact startups were very strong on their purpose, but lacked skills on the business side, and did not have the network to access mentors and experts. If that challenge was not addressed, they would always have a very hard time with their largest pain, to find funding.

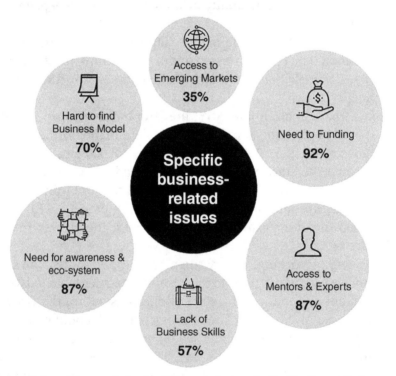

Source: Rainmaking analysis of +40 Impact startups in the Nordics on their business challenges, Q1 2018.

The Growth & Impact team decided to launch a digital platform; plusimpact.io is a free marketplace where impact startups could post a business challenge, e.g. review of business model, how to approach investors and communication, etc. Voluntary experts could then provide pro-bono advice to the startup.

In the beginning of 2019, the number of onboarded experts and the number of matches between impact startups and experts showed an exponential development. In April 2019, it had already reached the target of number of matches for the whole year. The interest from the experts, in particular, was high.

Focus now turned to increasing the number of impact startups to keep pace with the scaling of the expert and matches.

The numbers grew but kept being dependent on manual nudging of the startups, despite being a solution that was desirable for the startups on paper. At the time Nordic impact startups where matched with experts corresponding to more than three times a day and whilst it was practically feasible to do, it had not proved to be possible to find a viable solution to create a digital engine and scale it as a community-driven platform.

As a result, the +impact platform was refurbished in May 2020, focusing solely on connecting the impact startups with investors. With the changed focus, the platform today holds more than 1,000 impact startups across the Nordics and more than 400 investors, all having an interest in impact investments.

The +impact platform helps the startups to navigate through investment opportunities with the help of various tools, recommendations and funding overviews. As an impact investor, you can scout for startups that fit the portfolio and preferences within the sustainability areas, i.e. the UN Sustainable Development Goals.

As part of the +impact universe, the Nordic impact startups are also mapped as a group to provide data and insights back to the startup and investor community, all with a focus on helping accelerate progress in the Nordic impact startup ecosystem.

Since the beginning of the +impact initiative, the impact startup agenda has developed at amazing speed from a few converted believers to becoming a much more well-established sustainability and green transition trend. The bank continues to work on how to create an even stronger value proposition to the impact startup segment on the +impact platform, thereby maintaining a role of being the most comprehensive overview of the impact startups in the Nordics.

Experience from working with the impact startups has also spread into the other commercial units of the bank, inspiring advisors and business customers of how to work strategically and in practice with sustainability.

Delivery

The team, internal and external partners, funding and focus on execution have all been instrumental in delivering with speed to the underserved segment of startups and scaleups.

DB decided to move forward with a dedicated team that would serve the startup and scaleup segment with specialised knowledge within the segment needs.

In order to be able to execute with speed, the team behind Growth and Impact is a small Nordic team that uses external partners with the right competencies. The team has end-to-end ownership of the activities, which means they are themselves able to analyse the challenge, decide on the solution and execute it in the market without any dependencies to other teams in the bank and hence no delay during the process.

Within the impact sub-segment, for instance, this has been done by means of the +impact platform and also by creating a successful impact accelerator, by issuing reports on, for example, impact startups and investments, diversity and inclusion and overviews of the ecosystem.

In addition to the core team, there are 50+ Growth Advisors in Denmark, Sweden and Finland working closely with the team. They are located across the business and market areas of the bank and specialise in helping startups and growth companies.

When recruiting new people, the bank first had a top-down approach where local managers allocated resources to the growth advisors internally. It turned out not to be the most suitable way to proceed as it resulted in some people who were not truly motivated for the job.

To address this, they turned it upside down and learned that they needed a bottom-up approach, letting motivated people reach out to them. As a consequence, it has now become much easier to recruit new people to the team internally. This approach has secured passionate and personally motivated co-workers joining the team.

Another key factor for the success of the Growth & Impact teams has been to create strong relations and engagement with related units, such as Credit, Personal Banking and Private Banking. This is achieved not only by creating personal relations, but also engaging the people in understanding the special needs of startups, the new business models and to approach startups holistically, as a company and as a founder with specific personal demands, which the bank is able to fulfil, thanks to its size.

The budget is granted on a yearly basis to support the overall vision of helping startups to scale. The team is then responsible for deploying the budget in the most productive and efficient way. Again, this supports the mandate of end-to-end responsibility and enables the team to execute with speed, not having to wait for other priorities in the bank.

The budget was smaller than for other Moonshot projects in the bank, creating a strong focus on a lean setup and a focused product suite.

The Growth & Impact initiative is based on continuous learning and adaption. Therefore, the delivery has, accordingly, been in small steps moving closer to cover the whole scope of the problem as it is revealed. When working with an undefined problem you need to be able to work with speed and ask for validation from the market to get learnings. Keep having the 'problem to be solved' and not the 'product' as the guiding star for your development. You have to be ready to kill your darlings (the idea, the product) if feedback from the market is not positive. This has been the most prominent benefit of the chosen approach.

Results

'Another benefit we have seen is around employee engagement; if you find a bigger purpose of what you do, because you can see an alignment of your personal values and the work that you do, it is easier to attract and retain talent.'

Klavs Hjort, SVP and Head of Growth & Impact

From the very beginning, the overall vision of Danske Bank Growth & Impact and the measure of success is to 'Help startups scale their business'. This is still what they are working towards through all the initiatives they are driving.

The overall KPI is anchored in the long-term corporate strategy of the bank. As part of its impact on society, the bank has set the ambitious target of supporting 10,000 Nordics startups and scaleups with growth and impact tools, services and expertise, by 2023. By October 2020, 4,600+ startups or scaleups have been supported.

In addition to this KPI, operational targets are set annually and followed for each of the initiatives. The commercial results show in the startup and scaleup customer portfolios of the growth advisors. The ambition is to have 20% year-on-year (YoY) growth in income from the segment, which so far has been reached, showing a substantial success for the team.

Furthermore, along the way, the bank and commercial part of Growth & Impact have been on a journey to understand how fast-growing companies operate today. New ways of assessing risk and new ways of working have been the result.

Learnings

For the bank to find its role in catering for the startup and scaleup segment, it has been key to the Growth & Impact team to be an integrated part of the startup and impact startup ecosystem. In order to gain credibility and licence to speak within this specialised segment, that means not acting as a traditional bank, but as a startup bank that understands and solves the specific needs of startups and founders. That especially means being able to operate and think as a startup. To do so, they have learned the importance of these aspects:

- Have a strong mandate from management with end-to-end responsibility and a budget granted to support the overall vision. Leaving the team with the responsibility for deploying the budget in the most productive and efficient way, and enabling them to execute with speed.
- Be humble to your own limitation and be aware of the mindset you have as a bank and corporate. It is key to find the right partners with the right mindset and a stronghold in the ecosystem.
- Understand the problems the startups are truly facing, before rushing into what you foresee is the solution.
- Seek market validation. A key element to the agile approach is to launch with speed and have feedback loops based on validation from the segment.
- Be ready to kill your darlings and double down on what works. It is the validation from the startups and scaleups that needs to be decisive for what to change and not the internal perception.

What's Next

The approach and model of how the bank can cater for the startups and scaleup is by now tested and demonstrated to be viable towards the segment. The expectations for the next five years are to institutionalise the setup and scale the operation across all Nordic markets. Eventually it will, as the startups turn into the big companies of the future, be the normal way of operating as a bank.

Furthermore, it will be important in the coming years to continue aligning with the rest of the bank and integrate the unit 'back into the Bank', e.g. by exploring how to create a value proposition towards other customer groups in the bank that find it attractive to establish relations with startups. For corporate customers it will centre around collaborating with startups on new

launch it at the same time. This would create recognition and make it easy for customers to understand and learn from one another. Here the project quickly ran into its next big challenge. Since the decision of a one app strategy was taken late in the project the front-end development of the UX for the app was rushed and when tested on customers it was clear that the UX did not meet customers' expectations. Rebuilding the app would jeopardise the time plans and increase the cost for the project. The project was not unified in what way to take one part of the project, as it was more focused on the technical part of the project it wanted to proceed without changes to meet deadlines and budget, while another part of the project was business and brand and wanted to ensure that the product was delivering on customer expectation. The project went back to the set ambition, to create the simplest solution on the market, and decided to risk the time plan to ensure that the product lived up to that ambition. The whole front-end part of the app was redone and even this challenge caused a lot of fractions within the project at the time but it made the project stronger and brought tech and business closer for the rest of the project.

However, even a brilliant technical solution that is easy to use for everyone is worthless if it does not spread. The banks accordingly agreed on certain important principles:

- Creating high levels of recognition
- Ensuring massive spread
- Minimising support

The banks decided, in order to create recognition and ensure widespread penetration, that they would build on the network effect and social media. This would be a service where the customers could learn from one another and where recognition was spread from one sector of the public to another. The banks accordingly selected specific situations where the service could be of real benefit and appointed ambassadors who could spread app recognition amongst other users.

The name of the service was important too, but the banks all had different naming principles and there were numerous suggestions.

After many lengthy discussions, however, and a thorough market survey, they opted for what had actually been the project's working name: Swish. This simple name has also proven to be a real factor for success, and the verb 'to Swish', has even been added to the Swedish Academy's Glossary of the Swedish language.

An in-depth programme was also initiated with the aim of developing a logo that reflected the strength inherent in the fact that Swish was a joint solution. The different colours in the logo represent the different banks and the white field in the middle represents togetherness.

Delivery

'Six of the largest banks doing something together should be impossible, but since the team was able to put their corporate hat to the side, and put on their new Swish hat, we created a great culture of working together.'

Carl Molinero, Head of the Swedbank Pay and Chairman
of the Board, Swish

The banks are not allowed to collaborate on offering or price and any development of Swish must, therefore, be conducted in parallel by all six banks, and the respective providers of the Swish system, the Swish app, and the clearing and settlement system.

Everything was done at the same time in accordance with the waterfall methodology. Some banks acted as friendly banks, i.e. they were prepared to test and run through the entire system before the others, but the actual launch would be simultaneous. The system and acceptance testing was rigorous as it involved transferring money between different individuals. Everything had to work from the very first payment. The banks would implement an enormous testing schedule, ending with stress testing to ensure how much the system could handle.

Swedbank acted as the lead bank and had to move away from waterfall to agile to deliver this on time. With a very open mind and willingness to be in front of this project Swedbank decided to set up one team with business and IT working together using agile methods, with short sprints, daily meetings and incremental planning. Without this commitment from management, and the funding in place, this would not have worked.

In December of 2012 the first version of Swish for payments between private individuals was launched. Of importance – all banks had their own customer offering and Swedbank had to choose to price the service. Since pricing is very sensitive Swedbank built the decision on customer surveys with both unique interviews and large surveys. The outcome was clear and showed that as many as 75% were willing to pay for the service. Swedbank felt fully prepared; Swish did, after all, meet a real customer need. However, after massive pressure, particularly from journalists, regarding the pricing the price was changed the very next day to zero.

The fact that Swish was a free service helped ensure enormous levels of interest. Private individuals could now send money between each other in real time, 24/7/365. This was something completely new and absolutely fantastic, and it was free of charge. Swish was soon a massive success, and apart from customer satisfaction the solution has contributed to reduce the cost and use of cash.

Customers immediately started submitting new wish lists and new ideas on how Swish could be used in more ways and more situations. This drove the development of Swish for companies and in June 2014, Swish for Corporate (C2B) was launched as a simple, basic service that enabled private individuals to pay a company via Swish, by entering an alias (Swish number). Corporate customers could now get paid by Swish (an account-to-account transfer) in real time. It works around the clock, throughout the year.

The business model was built on a four-corner-model, and all six banks launched the service simultaneously with their own customer offering and pricing. It became apparent, this time, that there was an acceptance of charging and a willingness to pay on the part of corporate clients. The number of affiliated companies consequently grew rapidly and Swish was also a hit with companies.

Swish became so popular that corporate customers began their own innovative processes and developed their own technical solutions, enabling them to accept payments via Swish. Companies were keen to reach as many payers as possible and to receive payment in real time, and it also became important to be able to say, 'we accept Swish'. Unfortunately, this innovation work contravened established regulations and had to be terminated, but the participating banks began, instead, reviewing the options for adapting the service in line with corporate customers' needs. This led to the start of the next stage; the development of a more digitised and automated service that could be integrated with the companies' own systems. This would create a system of secure and safe e-commerce payments in real time, with proof of guaranteed payment in conjunction with the purchase.

Therefore, in early 2016, it was time for the launch of Swish for Merchant (C2B adapted for e-commerce). Swish for Merchant would become the new way of paying directly and simply, and could reduce retailers' concerns in connection with bank payments at that time, which were based on interbank solutions.

Retailers had previously needed to open accounts and sign agreements with multiple banks and had to deal with cumbersome administration and reconciliation, due to incoming transactions on different accounts in different banks, and a variety of reports. Swish for Merchant would eliminate the need for any of this. All the retailer needed was one account with one bank to receive a guaranteed payment. This would improve liquidity and give the retailers a better overview of and control over their finances.

Payments have also been simplified over the years. In 2016, for example, QR codes were launched for all users, and 2020 saw the launch of the sought-after 'Requests' function that enables users to send friends and acquaintances reminders about a Swish payment.

In 2020 Swish has also piloted Swish Payouts, which allows merchants to make instant payouts to their private customers.

Results

Almost 80% of the Swedish population now use Swish and 230,000 companies accept it. The number of users is continuing to grow across all age groups. The fact that the service is so easy to understand and use has meant that it has had a higher average age than other payment solutions.

Swish's success has also been reflected in the number of awards it has received since its launch. Swish has been voted the most meaningful digital brand in Sweden for several years now, beating both Google and Spotify. In both 2019 and 2020, Swish was declared the industry's most sustainable brand by the Sustainable Brand Index. Swish has also, for several years now, been ranked in the top three on the list of popular brands.

The fact that a verb has also been created from the service, 'to Swish', and that this word has now been included in the Swedish Academy's Glossary of the Swedish language, must also be seen as proof of the service's popularity.

Lessons Learned

One important and fundamental factor behind the success of Swish is that the banks, despite their different DNA, size, and domestic markets, successfully united under a single brand and cooperated across boundaries. There have, of course, been different views along the way but in the end all banks set their individual corporate hats aside and came together under a shared umbrella. This is an important lesson to carry forward into future projects.

The partnership must also be based on a genuine customer need and everyone must have something to gain from it. One of the challenges faced in the work on Swish was that all the banks were different in style and size so they all agreed upfront that everyone would be treated the same. The banks have worked as a single team towards the same goal, been transparent and shared information with one another. Openness and trust are both important ingredients when working towards a common goal.

Rules that clearly define where collaboration is possible and permitted are also a must. It was important, during the entire Swish developmental process, to keep in mind that the partnership involved the infrastructure and that the banks were not allowed to cooperate on offerings and pricing.

Another influential factor in Swish's success was that, right from the start, the banks created a virtual organisation with clear delimitations of responsibility. This organisation was maintained throughout the process and partly continues to this day, within the collaboration process set up and run by Getswish AB.

Creating a shared brand was critical to get mass adoption and to get developers interested in building on the platform compared to each bank doing their own thing.

What's Next

The three services were launched in close cooperation between the owner banks, and the company was primarily run throughout by allocating resources from the banks to several working groups.

Today, Swish operates as a standalone business, with its own CEO and resources to continue driving the development of Swish's infrastructure and carry both the company and the Swish products forward.

The road ahead is clear: by understanding, listening to and learning from the market, Swish will continue to develop secure and relevant services for the future.

Chapter 14
Standard Chartered Partnering with other corporates

Case: Mox

Executive Summary

Hong Kong is the second largest banking market in the world. From a scale and profitability perspective, it is hugely important to the Standard Chartered Group (SC). Last year, the bank's retail operations in Hong Kong added close to US$600 million in pre-tax profit to the bank.

Executives at the bank asked themselves how they could remain competitive given the growing threat from digital non-bank players such as Alibaba and Tencent and also deepen their market share, particularly in the mass market.

SC made the decision to invest in a separate virtual bank, independent of its incumbent model based on their view on the future of banking and the opportunities and gaps they saw in the Hong Kong retail banking market. Mox by SC was launched in September 2020.

The 'build and buy' approach for third party services works well for Mox as it allows it to source from the best in the industry while also being able to create in-house where its own expertise is strongest. The Joint Venture approach with PCCW, HKT and Trip.com has also proven to be successful as it allows Mox to tap a customer base that is open to integrating banking with other services using digital-only channels.

As of December 2020, Mox had more than 66,000 customers with an average deposit size of US$9,000, totalling more than US$600 million in deposits.

Introductions

Do you want more details about this case? Find additional highlights from these interviews at www.howbanksinnovate.com.

Samir Subberwal, Managing Director and Head of Consumer, Private and Business Banking for Asia

Samir has been with the bank for over 20 years, focused on the Retail Banking business. Samir is responsible for business strategy, delivering financial performance, business efficiency and the bank's digital agenda. Samir holds an MBA from the University of Missouri-Kansas City.

Alex Manson, Head of Standard Chartered Ventures

Alex looks after SC Ventures at SC, which leads innovation and promotes intrapreneurship across the bank, invests in fintech companies and explores new business models with new disruptive ventures. Alex was previously Global Head of Transaction Banking, where he repositioned the business to a sustainable and growing franchise. He joined the bank as Group Head, Wholesale Banking Geographies in 2012. His roles at Deutsche Bank and Credit Suisse for 12 years spanned product and client coverage in New York, London, Frankfurt, Zurich, Hong Kong and Singapore. Alex holds an MBA from INSEAD.

Deniz Güven, CEO, Mox

Deniz is leading the team that is bringing a new way of banking to Hong Kong, by empowering people to grow and unlock possibilities through a truly digital and personalised banking experience. Mox operates in a whole new way by listening to customers and focusing on heart share. Deniz joined SC in 2017 as the Global Head, Design and Client Experience, where he oversaw client journey and optimizations, digital wealth and collaborations with tech firms and startups. Prior to joining SC, Deniz served as the Senior Vice President at BBVA Group's Garanti Bank in Turkey. During his role at Garanti, Deniz was responsible for end-to-end digital assets, as well as iGaranti, the only mobile bank in Turkey. Deniz holds an MBA from Istanbul Bilgi University.

Background

Key Figures

Total assets: US$720 billion
Number of customers: 14 million
Number of branches: 1,200
Number of full-time employees: 85,000
(Approximate as of 2020)

Standard Chartered (SC) is listed on the London and Hong Kong Stock Exchanges and has a presence in 60 markets and services customers across 150 markets worldwide.

Their emerging affluent clients and high net worth clients are serviced by the Retail and Private Banking business and their companies through our Corporate, Commercial and Institutional Banking business.

SC believes the future is full of opportunities but they must re-wire how they deliver financial services to both people and companies to remain relevant. They have defined three pillars to this strategy:

- **Innovation from outside.** Through innovation, fintech investment and SC Ventures, the bank has engaged with fintech companies for POCs and successfully implemented projects into production. They have launched SC Ventures fintech Bridge, a platform to connect community builders such as startups, investors and accelerators to the bank. They also take minority stakes in fintechs that they have done POCs with. SC believes they can help the startup grow sustainably and the startup can keep the bank nimble and agile.

- **Innovation from the inside.** Some of the best ideas can come from people working within the systems. As the team knows what works well and what needs fixing, particularly in terms of products, processes and the overall customer experience. The bank has eXellerator labs in multiple markets for client co-creation and to encourage internal innovation in Shanghai, Singapore, Hong Kong, London, Nairobi and San Francisco. The SC Innovate Ideation Platform and Intrapreneur Program nurture ideas from within their talent pool. Some of the ideas may become independent businesses and some might turn into products that the bank sells. The programme allows people to differentiate themselves as innovators and intrapreneurs, identifying the next generation of leaders within the business.

- **Ventures.** These are independent from the bank and allow the bank to experiment with new business models. In practice, several different disruptive business models have emerged. The first virtual bank Mox by SC was launched as a separate entity in Hong Kong in September 2020, joining the first eight virtual banks to disrupt the island's banking landscape. SC is administering the ecosystem and build platforms for market places with open connectivity. In India they launched Solv, a digital market place to help Small and Medium Enterprises (SMEs) grow their network within a supply chain ecosystem. The bank is currently building nexus, their banking as a service platform, that can be plugged into other platforms. This is a model where they build and own the back-end infrastructure but the customer face is owned by their social media or e-commerce ecosystem partners. The bank has also launched Zodia, in partnership with Northern Trust, as an institutional grade digital asset custodian service.

Problem

'Whilst most banks claimed to be omni-channel, there was a huge gap with regards to real end-to-end digital banks in HK.'

Samir Subberwal, Managing Director and Head of Consumer,
Private and Business Banking for Asia

Hong Kong is the second largest banking market in the world. From a scale and profitability perspective, it is hugely important to the Standard Chartered Group. Last year, the bank's retail operations in Hong Kong added close to US$600 million in pre-tax profit to the bank.

Looking ahead, executives at the bank asked themselves how they could remain competitive given the growing threat from digital non-bank players such as Alibaba and Tencent and also deepen their market share, particularly in the mass market. At the same time, customers increasingly want to integrate their banking with other services for a more seamless experience.

Stakeholders from across the bank's Retail Banking, Technology, Innovation and Strategy teams from a group, regional and country level came together to make Mox a reality, to address gaps in the market and the threat from digital competitors.

When identifying the problem or the opportunity for a virtual bank, Standard Chartered saw that their customer base was mostly in the affluent segment, with an average age of 45, so they were missing out on a huge mass market, particularly people under the age of 35. Then the bank looked at digital banking in Hong Kong overall, which considering the size of the market and its profitability, was very low. Taxis still operate on cash and cheques are still very much used, which gives a sense of how the market lags behind in digital adoption.

After more than 2,000 ethnographic studies in the Hong Kong market, SC decided a virtual bank could address many customer problems that were uncovered. The availability of convenient digital banking apps, easy account opening, particularly for expats, and financial planning for the future. Product sophistication in Hong Kong is very high but the actual digital or client experience focus was barely visible in the mobile banking and digital adoption rates, which presents a huge opportunity for digital financial services to provide.

In 2018, when the Hong Kong Monetary Authority (HKMA) first decided to issue licenses for virtual banks in a move to ramp up innovation in the banking sector, SC was among the first to apply and successfully receive one.

There were clearly two camps within the organisation. There were those who saw it as an opportunity and recognised the huge potential it presented, while those opposed felt that SC, as an incumbent, should just focus on innovation and bring their online offering to a new level. They did have many digital capabilities, a strong customer base and, as one of the note-issuing banks, an extensive branch network and a strong brand.

However, given the very real challenge to traditional banking models, the bank decided to proceed with the Mox concept, disrupting their existing model and attacking a new market with a completely digital one.

Solution

'Building a new venture is hard, so make sure you have a very committed CEO and significant backing from the wider executive team to buy you time to do it well, because you'll only get one chance to get it right once you launch.'

Alex Manson, Head of Standard Charter Ventures

SC made the decision to invest in a separate virtual bank, independent of its incumbent model and based on their view on the future of banking and the opportunities and gaps they saw in the Hong Kong retail banking market. Mox by Standard Chartered was launched in September 2020. Stakeholders agreed that the virtual bank was the right move to remain relevant in the future and also to solve many of the customer pain points that the bank's ethnographic research conducted with 2,000 people had revealed.

The bank decided to create Mox as a joint venture, keeping in mind that their view of the future was that banking would be an integrated one, with many different services, both in terms of infrastructure and delivery. Collaboration and partnerships are central to the Mox concept. It focuses on providing services not products. Core to the founding themes of Mox is the importance of creating customer 'ecosystems' linking together various customer needs. As such, the bank decided to partner with communications service providers, HKT and PCCW, given that their penetration of mobile and broadband services in the market was the largest among their peers at 40%, offering a massive existing mobile-friendly customer base to Mox. Trip.com, Asia's largest travel booking service, was also selected as one of the partners in the joint venture. On average, people in Hong Kong travel 4.2 times a year, so a partnership with a travel portal was a choice aligned with customer preferences. As a result, SC holds 65.1% in the joint venture, while PCCW, HKT and Trip.com hold 10.0%, 15.0% and 9.9% respectively.

Mox also works along a 'buy plus build' model, which means they are set up to source best-in-breed services from third parties. Like other neo banks, a point of advantage is that Mox is a 'cloud-native' bank, which allows it to integrate with third parties faster. The cloud-based infrastructure gave the bank the agility to quickly develop and deliver products and services.

Following guidance from the HKMA, Mox was first launched to 2,000 customers as a pilot and then to more in phases. As of December 2020, Mox had more than 66,000 customers with more than US$600 million in deposits, far surpassing the benchmarks set by existing digital and virtual banks across the world according to SC estimates. Customers have displayed a high level of trust in Mox, vis-à-vis what is seen in other similar ventures, as demonstrated in the average deposit size of US$9,000. The Mox team believes this early success has come from their mindset, which is to win 'share of heart' rather than 'share of wallet'. They look at adding value through services that address customer pain points: for instance, the team's KPI is to open accounts for customers as fast as possible, instead of a target number of accounts. With this approach, their fastest account opening logged is 2 minutes 47 seconds.

The concept of a virtual bank was new to not just the market but also to people involved in the Mox build. The team takes a proactive approach to educating both internally and externally about how a virtual bank works and the benefits it offers both to clients and in terms of a viable, profitable business model that can be scaled. Externally, Mox did not engage in above-the-line marketing, relying more on digital marketing and word-of-mouth to build its customer base. The 'Founding Member' programme, where the first batch of customers to sign up to Mox received a metal card, was a hugely successful campaign that saw more than 10,000 sign-ups in less than 24 hours. It helped build a sense of pride in the first customers, who then spread the word amongst their peers.

The Mox team is not innovating in isolation, but focuses on something SC calls 'micro innovation', which is essentially innovation in the services delivered to customers to make them fit more neatly into their lives and address their needs. They look at spending and saving as two sides of the same coin, rather than different products, as banks typically do. For example, when a customer deposits money, they earn a daily rate of interest. This does away with the myth that you can only earn interest on large sums. When they spend on their debit cards, the cash-back is delivered directly to their savings accounts.

Delivery

'We did a lot of market research to make sure the end-product would resonate with the audience. We moved away from traditional segmentation of age and income and focused entirely on data, grouping people by their actual behaviours.'

Deniz Güven, CEO, Mox

Mox started with an MVP concept, aligned with the HKMA guidance. After opening up to the first 2,000 customers in a closed launch, it went to market. For external awareness, Mox followed an advocacy model, using word-of-mouth and digital channels instead of above the line marketing. It is now the highest rated financial services in Hong Kong, rated at 4.8 (the average is between 2 and 3).

The 'build and buy' approach for third party services works well for Mox as it allows it to source from the best in the industry while also being able to create in-house where its own expertise is strongest. The Joint Venture approach with PCCW, HKT and Trip.com has also proven to be successful as it allows Mox to tap a customer base that is open to integrating banking with other services, using digital-only channels.

Mox is a fully cloud-native bank, operating on a core tech platform built in collaboration with some of the world's leading organisations and fintechs, allowing for the following cutting-edge services to be delivered to customers in Hong Kong:

- An AWS cloud-based virtual infrastructure and DevOps methods to deliver an integrated banking solution and enable delivery at pace.
- A smart contract model, connected with APIs. This reduces the number of layers in the banking system and increases speed, security/compliance and accuracy.
- Co-creation: harnessing the power of the entire Mox ecosystem to accelerate development and source best-in-class capabilities.
- A near real-time data catalogue on an event-driven architecture to ensure continuous compliance and strong data governance.
- A fast and personalised customer experience.

The above technology has enabled SC to deliver a world-class customer experience. Benefits to customers include:

- All-in-one numberless bank cards, enhancing privacy and security.
- The first virtual bank in Hong Kong to support both Apple Pay and Google Pay.

- Fast onboarding: Using a selfie and basic ID, customers can open an account in under three minutes, the fastest onboarding journey in the sector.
- Security: strong encryption, biometric login, Lost Wallet and e-Commerce Fraud Protection. Customers can also freeze or activate their card with one tap.
- Personalisation and engagement: customers can set up saving goals and pay/receive money from anyone, anytime in Hong Kong.
- Monitoring of real-time account activity and balance with instant categorisation.

Results

Mox was built in an extremely short timeframe from receiving its banking license in March 2019 to officially launching in September 2020. It was able to achieve a number of 'industry-firsts' for a virtual bank in the region, which aided the progress of its delivery to customers. These include the first numberless all-in-one bank card, the first virtual bank to do both Apple and Google Pay, the first to offer daily interest, the first to offer cash-back credits to bank accounts to offer the opportunity to earn interest, one of the first cloud data banks and the first virtual bank to hit 50k customers of more than 100 nationalities, a testament to its wide appeal.

Its success is reflected in multiple metrics. As at 31 December 2020, in just 100 days of operations, Mox has more than 66,000 customers with over US$600 million in customer deposits, far surpassing the benchmarks set by existing digital and virtual banks across the world, according to SC estimates. Customers have displayed a high level of trust in Mox, vis-à-vis what is seen in other similar ventures, as demonstrated in the average deposit size of around US$10,000. Customer feedback has also been very strong with an App Store rating of 4.8 out of 5 and Google Play rating of 4.7 out of 5 as at 31 December 2020, making Mox the highest rated and most reviewed virtual bank app in Hong Kong on the App Store and Google Play. With a focus on speed, instead of a target number of accounts, their fastest account opening logged is 2 minutes 47 seconds. The median account opening time is under 8 minutes.

The joint venture approach has also proved to be very success-ful. Their partnership with telecommunications service providers, HKT and parent PCCW with their 40% plus penetration of mobile and broadband services in the market, offered a massive existing mobile-friendly customer base to Mox. Trip.com, Asia's largest online travel booking service, are already well-integrated in the lifestyles of the target clients, helping Mox reach unprecedented numbers in both client onboarding and deposit size.

Learnings

A key challenge was hiring the right talent at the right time.

People with specialist finance and technology skills were both hard to find in Hong Kong, so some senior positions had to be filled from overseas. Starting with a mere three-person team, Mox now employs more than 180 people who represent 28 different national-ities, bringing an exciting level of diversity to the workplace.

Governance also posed some learning as Mox was linked to Standard Chartered plc. Its governance structure could not be in isolation from the Standard Chartered Group so the team had to create an acceptable balance of independence and control within a unique matrix governance structure. It is vital to have a very committed CEO, who can help launch with buy-in from key stakeholders in the incumbent organisation, in this case, Standard Chartered Bank.

Mox was built in an extremely short timeframe with most of the team working remotely for most of the time. It is essential to have a team that can adapt to changing circumstances and work with a high level of agility.

Most importantly, it is essential to understand the clients they are trying to reach, with a high level of depth. Over 2,000 Hong Kong people were engaged in the ethnographic studies and this allowed them to identify exactly what customers were lacking in the

Hong Kong market and based on this information they were able to 'micro-innovate' to deliver products and solutions that resonate with the target demographic. A large part of their success was due to the fact that they stepped away from the traditional definitions of banking products, for instance the separation of spending and savings products at traditional banks. They chose to go with an approach from a customer's point of view to develop an integrated spending and savings solution, where anything spent on a credit card will earn cash back directly in the savings account, which in turn will grow with the application of a daily rate of interest. Building a bank from the ground up has been a rewarding and fulfilling experience for the team. We highlight below some of our key lessons learned:

- **Building a blueprint.** Being the first venture in SC to build an entirely cloud native bank from the ground up has meant a lot of test-and-learn for both Mox and SC. Without a clearly defined template for building a virtual bank, they encountered and overcame a lot of unknowns together, especially at the onset. This did impact their delivery timelines from initial plans and did require additional headcount and cost to overcome. They now have far fewer unknowns than when they first started, and future ventures would benefit from the template/blueprint developed by Mox.
- **Talent.** Assembling the right team to build a virtual bank in HK has been a challenge, especially having the right talents/teams at the right time. They were unsuccessful at times in recruiting the best talent they had interviewed. There continues to be a scarcity of local talent who have experience building and running digital banks, and the global and local situations added to the risk and mobility of talents.
- **Organisational maturity.** Mox has matured significantly from a handful of people to over 180 people. Having the right people, at the right time, focused on the right priorities is critical.

What's Next

As of December 2020, Mox offers accounts with saving, spend and payments products. Looking ahead, Mox plans to expand its product suite and also aggressively build up its market share. The initial results have been very encouraging and Mox will look to accelerate this momentum in 2021, where it aims to launch new products and services. A number of services including its credit card are already in beta testing with customers and is expected to launch shortly.

In addition to Mox, Standard Chartered is focusing on multiple disruptive ventures via its SC Ventures arm, which has already rolled out a number of successes. In India they launched Solv, a digital marketplace to help Small and Medium Enterprises (SMEs) grow their network within a supply chain ecosystem. The bank is currently building nexus, their banking as a service platform, which can be plugged into other platforms. This is a model where they build and own the back-end infrastructure but the customer face is owned by their social media or e-commerce ecosystem partners. The bank has also launched Zodia, in partnership with Northern Trust, as an institutional grade digital asset custodian service.

Part IV

Bonus: Ways of Working

Chapter 15
N26
Ways of Working

Case: Tech Hubs

N̄26

Executive Summary

In order to become the bank that 100 million people around the world love to use, N26 needed to grow its customer base, expand in new markets, launch new innovative products, develop its IT infrastructure and, to do so, recruit at speed, gathering the best minds in product and tech from all over the world to take the company on this journey to disrupt an industry.

Yet, being able to attract top talent in a hypercompetitive environment at both scale and speed meant looking beyond simply coming to the table with a compelling job offer. While many of the world's most qualified talents were willing to relocate, very often, where they were moving to was often just as important as the opportunity they were moving for.

N26 approached this by investing in two new Tech Hubs in Europe, expanding their presence outside of their home city of Berlin to Barcelona and Vienna. This approach allowed them to focus on the long-term priority of expanding their product capabilities and team, attracting talent from all around the world with a selection of relocation opportunities in cities offering very different experiences and lifestyles depending on one's life priorities.

Opened between 2018 and 2019, the two Tech Hubs today have played critical roles in driving many of the recent features and functionalities that have made it to market as part of an expanded and improved N26 digital banking experience, and will continue to be crucial pillars of the digital bank's innovation strategy now and in the future.

Introductions

Do you want more details about this case? Find additional highlights from these interviews at www.howbanksinnovate.com.

Valentin Stalf, Founder and CEO

Valentin founded N26 in 2013 with his longtime friend Maximilian Tayenthal. He is today the CEO of the digital bank aiming to disrupt an industry ripe for change. Valentin is an entrepreneur at heart, with a passion for solving problems with technology. Before N26, he was an Entrepreneur in Residence for Rocket Internet, an incubator and investor in online startups. Valentin has a Bachelor's degree in Business Administration and Management and a Master's degree in Accounting and Finance from the University of St Gallen. He is also a member of the advisory board at the Vienna University of Economics and Business.

Georg Hauer, General Manager of N26 in Germany, Austria, Switzerland and Northern Europe

Georg is the General Manager of N26 in Germany, Austria, Switzerland (DACH) and Northern Europe. Additionally, he also oversees N26's TechHub in Vienna. With deep experience in scaling global challenger brands, Georg joined N26 in March 2018 as the General Manager of Austria. Prior to N26, he was a General Manager at Uber and a management consultant at the Boston Consulting Group with a focus on technology and digitalisation. Georg holds an MBA from the Kellogg School of Management in Chicago and a degree from the Vienna University of Economics and Business.

Francisco Sierra, General Manager Spain

Francisco joined N26 in 2018 as General Manager Spain and is responsible for growing the digital bank's key offer and presence in the Spanish market. He is also Director of European Markets at N26, with the mission of tailoring a global strategy for local success.

Francisco has more than ten years of experience in banking and financial services. He started his career in investment banking at J.P. Morgan, before moving on to venture capital at Active Venture Partners and Funding Circle as Managing Director of Spain and Head of Strategy and Business Operations for the US market.

He studied Industrial Engineering at ICAI and he holds an MBA at IESE Business School.

Background

Key Figures

Total Assets: n/a
Number of customers: 7 million
Number of branches: n/a
Number of employees: 1,500
(Approximate as of 2020)

N26 was founded in 2013 by longtime friends Valentin Stalf (CEO) and Maximilian Tayenthal (CFO) who, frustrated by the lack of transparency, digital innovation and personalised offerings at traditional banks, decided to build their own with a vision to deliver a new type of banking experience. They designed N26 to be a customer-centric retail bank that would completely reimagine banking for the smartphone, allowing anyone to enjoy an elegant and easy-to-use banking app that would make it possible to manage money on a 100% digital platform.

In an industry that has too often been institutional, dysfunctional and complex for many, N26 set out to offer a banking experience to empower everyone to live and bank their way. The app is centred around the customer experience and integrates the most innovative technology to make the life of the modern customer easier.

N26's name draws inspiration from the Rubik Cube, which is made up of 26 smaller cubes. Solving this infamous 3D puzzle is complex, but once one knows the right sequence of moves and strategies to tackle it, it becomes simple and straightforward. N26's goal was to apply the same approach to banking, which has historically been a complex and sometimes frustrating consumer experience that lacks simple, elegant solutions. With the right approach and combination of moves, N26 wanted to make banking fundamentally better.

N26 did not originally start out as a fully-fledged bank. The very first product was launched in cooperation with a banking partner that provided the necessary infrastructure and regulatory framework. From the successful initial launch, knowing that there was demand in the market for a simple and mobile-first banking experience, N26's founders made the ambitious decision to build their own bank and apply for a full banking license.

Since the founders launched the initial product back in early 2015, the company has grown to over 7 million customers around the world, and is present in 25 global markets, with its largest markets being Germany, Austria, France, Spain, Italy and the United States.

Today, N26 has over 1,500 employees from around the world and is built by engineers, programmers, designers, copywriters, analysts, customer care agents, lawyers, researchers, statisticians, marketeers and bankers. N26's employees represent a diverse group made up of 80 nationalities, and the diversity of the company's employee base is valued as a major source of strength, allowing it to draw from a wealth of creativity, perspectives and experiences to help deliver the most relevant and inclusive product to customers globally.

Problem

'If you want to build a global technology organisation, you need to become a global technology organisation, and that starts with your people.'

Georg Hauer, General Manager in Germany, Austria,
Switzerland and Northern Europe

Since the launch of N26's first product in 2015, N26 has had the ambition to become not only a global company but also a global employer. In order to become the bank that 100 million people around the world love to use, N26 needed to invest heavily in expanding in new markets, launching new, innovative products, and developing its IT infrastructure with the goal to scale. To do this, one thing was certain: N26 had to scale up product and technology teams, and fast.

With its headquarters in Berlin, the growing digital bank was already one of the biggest and most well-known tech employers in the city. Even though the company was continuing to bring on board top talent from across the city, country and indeed the globe, this was still not enough to keep pace with N26's growth ambitions. N26's efforts to scale up its team saw the digital bank's workforce of just a few hundred employees grow dramatically, sometimes at the rate of over 100 new employees a month. It became obvious that in order to open up new opportunities to attract top talent, N26 would have to expand its horizons beyond the city it called home.

Thanks to its already extremely international workforce, N26 was well aware of how important office locations can be when factoring into an international candidate's decision to accept a new position and relocate. With this, the management made the decision to establish a new presence outside of Berlin over expanding the company's presence in the city, in order to be able to tap into new talent pools and present a more compelling and flexible offer to prospective candidates.

With the most pressing business need being to accelerate the delivery of product innovation at the highest standard, exploring a setup that would centre on speed and autonomy was key. Instead of approaching this as an outsourcing hub for routine tasks, the solution had to bolster the company's capabilities by driving strategic, high-impact output. A Tech Hub was the perfect solution.

A new Tech Hub would present a scalable opportunity to incubate ideas and innovation, allowing operational teams to deliver product innovation at pace, owning the process in-house from start to finish. To do this, N26 worked to implement a solution that would see the company build new teams of product managers, product designers, front-end and back-end developers, engineer managers, etc., who would be able to execute to the same quality and speed as those in the company's Berlin headquarters.

In addition, venturing outside of Berlin would provide a new dimension to lean on when working to attract talent in Europe's competitive tech community, opening up further opportunities to look beyond what a company offered as an employer, but what a city offered as a place to relocate and create new life experiences. By opening up a whole new range of cultural backdrops to suit different lifestyle preferences and life stages, N26 hoped that looking outside of its existing base in Berlin would allow them to offer something compelling to the world's top tech talent, no matter their backgrounds, priorities and hopes for their next big career opportunity.

Solution

'While Silicon Valley has always been seen as the global home of big tech companies, N26 is committed to expanding our investments across Europe. We believe that N26 can play a significant role in building world-class innovation hubs and technical capabilities right here in Europe.'

Valentin Stalf, Founder and CEO

N26 addressed this by opening two new Tech Hubs in Europe. With the growing pace of growth within the business and yet more ambitious plans for the future creating increasing pressure to scale product and tech capabilities to match the needs of a global technology leader, it was clear that it would have to approach this as much more than a simple hiring and expansion job.

With these goals in mind, N26 approached the decisions on which cities to establish its new presence in by conducting rigorous analysis on over 10 countries/cities, using a mix of quantitative and qualitative criteria from sources that included desk research (reports from consultancy firms, global and local observatories and statal sources, qualitative rankings) and one-to-one interviews with other leaders from other companies in the start-up space, covering topics ranging from the cost of living to the complexity of applying for employment visas for non-European employees and their family members.

A selection of cities was evaluated based on a myriad of qualitative and quantitative factors to eventually get a single numerical score. These included:

- Cost of living and purchasing power index
- Standard of living index
- Convenience factors such as cost and proximity to transportation and distance from the nearest international airport
- Size of the product and tech talent pool
- Access to top-ranked universities with world-leading tech programmes
- Visa application complexity
- Friendliness towards English speakers
- Rental prices
- Number of engineers per open role
- Number of technical graduates per 1,000 inhabitants
- Time differences from the headquarters in Berlin
- Flight prices and available connections for inter-office travel
- Number of startups/size of startup ecosystem
- Number and size of VC firms established in the city
- Rate of growth of the local startup ecosystem

Barcelona, known for its vibrant tech ecosystem and fast-growing investment landscape, proved to be an immediate fit, ranking strongly in the majority of the categories evaluated. Considered among Europe's top five cities for developing startups in 2018 according to a study by EU-startup published annually that evaluated Europe's biggest startup hubs, it unsurprisingly attracted over 58% of Spain's international investment, with 55% of startups in Barcelona's ecosystem working on app-based businesses. In addition, there was a steady inflow of global talent into Barcelona's tech scene, thanks to two internationally renowned technological universities and was ranked third in Europe as the preferred city for pursuing MBAs. The choice in this case was straightforward.

With this, N26 opened its first Tech Hub in Barcelona in 2018, with plans quickly underway to select and open a second one the following year. While many of Europe's most iconic cities made the list, many lost out due to high costs of living or potential challenges for talent who would not speak the local language. In this case, the two strong contenders emerged as the potential home of N26's third European base, Lisbon and Vienna.

Through a detailed feedback process and candidate interviews, N26's team discovered that most candidates considering Lisbon as a city to move to for work, were very often open to working in Barcelona as well. With the ability to attract diverse top talent, one of the key drivers of N26's decision in choosing the location of their second Tech Hub, Vienna, won out, and the Tech Hub there was opened in 2019 with many of the country's top personalities in business, government and society in attendance.

Beyond being voted the city with the world's highest quality of living for a decade, N26 already had a strong following in the city, thanks to the founders both being Austrian. The company was well-established within the city's startup and enterprise community, and its founders connected well with local media, politicians and business leaders, setting a strong foundation that would help the company quickly establish its physical presence in a city it already knew well.

Together, Berlin, Barcelona and Vienna, each vibrant startup cities with strong innovation ecosystems in their own right, allowed N26 to offer a variety of relocation options for candidates with diverse needs, priorities and life situations. From a cultural standpoint, the choice of three offices meant that new hires could choose between Berlin's great cost of living, edgy subculture and vibrant nightlife, Barcelona's southern cultural flair and cosmopolitan vibe, and Vienna's calm pace of living, open green spaces and rich history, which was perfect for families moving with children and partners. At the end of the day, this approach allowed N26 to expand its ability to attract talent by focusing not just on the standard factors influencing candidates on the specific professional opportunity, but also on the non-job-related aspects that came with accepting a position at N26 to come on board to build the bank the world loves to use.

Delivery

'Different cities appeal to different people, so by broadening our catchment area, we could find the very best talent out there and attract a much more diverse team.'

Francisco Sierra, General Manager Spain

After making the important decision on the cities the European Tech Hubs were to be based, the real work began to tackle three main priorities in each site:

- Choosing and constructing the new spaces
- Recruiting and building the local tech teams
- Creating strong links between the new Tech Hub teams and those based in the Berlin headquarters

N26's procurement teams evaluated a comprehensive criteria of selection requirements when exploring options for the locations of the bank's new Tech Hubs. Their criteria shortlisted office locations based on metrics such as rental prices and rates, minimum rental durations and contractual flexibility to account for scaling and pivoting as the company evolved as a fast-moving startup, proximity to the city centre and proximity to other startups or the city's innovation ecosystem.

The final criteria were particularly important given N26's focus on expanding N26's product and tech capabilities with these new hubs. N26 teams eventually landed on spaces at OneCowork in Barcelona's Plaça Catalunya, right in the heart of the city, sharing a building with numerous innovative companies, and at weXelerate in Vienna, an Innovation Hub that placed N26 in the same building as several startups and innovation departments of big tech corporations, helping to connect N26 better with the most creative and innovative minds in both cities.

In both new office sites, numerous considerations were taken into account in a central project plan in order to create a safe and compliant workspace that was optimised for innovation, collaboration and creativity. From registering local legal entities, conducting security risk assessments to the most stringent standards as a bank, and ensuring all safety guidelines and regulations were adhered to, to optimizing the setup of their IT infrastructure and consulting research and subject matter experts to create an office centred around occupational health and wellbeing, numerous cross-functional teams comprising members from within N26 as well as external partners worked to deliver both hugely complex projects on time, and on budget.

Given the complexity of the undertaking to establish the first N26's presence outside the home markets, N26 deployed cross-functional project management teams to deliver both projects, and defined a clear decision-making process using the RAPID methodology to ensure effective and efficient decision making in a complex stakeholder environment that would take on board not just quantitative criteria like cost, but qualitative ones as well.

Special attention was given to sustainability and responsible use, making sure that the investments could be scaled and re-used in case of moving to other offices. In Barcelona in particular, the team was also able to attain Platinum LEED certification for the office space.

With hiring new staff in the new locations the top priority, N26 looked to fill positions at the newly opened Tech Hubs the moment they were operationally ready to welcome N26's first employees. The focus was to be able to bring people on board at pace to have teams fully staffed and operational as soon as possible. With this came an unexpected challenge. The pool of junior candidates in the product and tech space in Europe was not only larger than the pool of senior candidates, but also significantly more geographically mobile. As a result, it was significantly easier to bring on board junior talent at speed, leaving gaps in the team at the senior level. Without senior engineers, developers and product owners in place, local teams continued to lack the necessary guidance, steer and direction in order to be fully autonomous and capable of delivering product innovations from start to finish. This led N26 to quickly adjust its approach to focus first on staffing more senior levels of the team, especially given the smaller size of the talent pool and high level of competition for qualified senior product and tech specialists.

Changing the approach to recruiting talent for the Tech Hubs to focus on senior hires first also helped N26 to ensure that leaders were able to build their teams and set the growth trajectory of their divisions in a way that made sense, rather than having junior teams on board required to deliver without senior expertise and guidance.

With N26's first overseas teams coming together in the Tech Hubs, ensuring a way to build meaningful connections and crucial cultural alignment between all teams was going to be critical for success. Tackling this challenge would help ensure a cohesive approach that would see initiatives and products delivered end-to-end in the Tech Hubs plugging in seamlessly into N26's product roadmap, and N26's main product innovations being able to be tackled efficiently and effortlessly across three fully functioning teams across different geographies with different areas of expertise.

As a company with digital in their DNA, N26 built a framework for effective remote collaboration between the three offices. Teams were in regular contact with the team in Berlin, with many team members being onboarded with new employees in the Berlin offices, and even travelling to the headquarters for key meetings and planning sessions, on top of regular remote meetings with the full product team across all three geographies. The balance of a heavy use of digital technology to facilitate remote collaboration, along with an investment in ensuring face time and knowledge sharing between colleagues in all offices helped set up a seamless and efficient rhythm of business between teams in all three locations.

Results

Both of N26's Tech Hubs in Barcelona and Vienna were launched in the attendance of the company's employees and senior stakeholders, including the founders and members of the N26 executive leadership team, as well as business leaders and prominent figures in the local startup ecosystem and local media.

Dedicated press events and outreach helped drive awareness and interest of N26 opening its new Tech Hub in each of the cities, helping to drive attention within the local and international business and tech community and a broader understanding of N26's overall vision and mission, and its commitment to investing in driving innovation in Europe.

Today, both Tech Hubs continue to be on a journey to scale up their staff strength, with the goal to eventually employ hundreds of tech and product experts between them. Yet, with barely a few years in operation, numerous important product features and innovations have already made their way from the Tech Hubs to the market. These included:

- Some of the brand's most well-loved features, such as Dark Mode
- Instant payment capabilities within the N26 app
- N26 You, one of the digital bank's premium subscription bank accounts
- The Perks Program launched in the US, a unique way to give account holders with an N26 debit card the same rewards and benefits that one would expect to see from a credit card provider

- Numerous security upgrades and feature updates that improved many of the product's functionalities under the hood to make managing money safer, easier and more seamless within the app

Additional first-time additions to the N26 product are also planned and slated for release in the coming year, which will expand the digital bank's customer offer beyond its existing services.

Learnings

In approaching the challenge of taking its ability to bring on the best global tech talent to a new level, N26 had to take a strategic yet granular approach with a focus on the big picture and how to achieve a long-term vision, alongside dedication to pay attention to even the smallest details.

Rather than looking to address the immediate pain point of needing to hire more people faster, N26 looked at the issue and how it would play out in a future where the company would continue growing, and do so faster than ever before. It considered solutions that would take time to put together and come at much greater complexity and cost, but would address long-term needs rather than immediate ones. The two-year exercise of opening two separate Tech Hubs in Europe not only underscored their commitment to Europe's innovation community, but helped address one of the challenges to hire top talent in an effective yet unconventional way by going to the cities that would give them the lifestyles they wanted for themselves.

On the other side of the scale, being able to analyze and consider the minute details from both an organizational point of view as a business, as well as a personal point of view as a normal person making the daily commute to work, and from the tangible to the less so. Like the impact of the types of furnishings on occupational health, N26 was able to take a holistic, informed and future-focused approach to expanding its presence across the European continent and pave the way for innovation at the company to continue to thrive.

What's Next

In the next 5–10 years, N26 is planning to bring its digital banking experience to customers in even more markets, like Brazil, and truly become the financial home for customers to connect their money to every other aspect of their life, all from the device in the palm of their hand.

These ambitious plans will require innovation on a few levels to expand the N26 product to eventually offer a complete range of financial services as a digital bank, to work with partners in the tech ecosystem to create a connected experience in a heavily regulated industry. As well as establishing a new business model within the world of banking that allows customers to create a banking experience built around their needs, thanks to value-added subscription-based accounts and add-on features in a freemium model like Spotify and Netflix today.

Central to this will be the ability for N26's product and tech teams to continue to drive innovation across the entire N26 digital banking experience at scale, while growing the supporting infrastructure as well as the relevance of the bank in all its markets with localised features and offerings as the offer continues to scale and grow. The digital bank already has plans to scale up its product team still further in the coming year, with the intention to bring on board over 200 additional product specialists as it doubles down on its investment in the talent required to drive change as a pioneer in the global banking industry.

Chapter 16
Royal Bank of Canada
Ways of Working

Case: NOMI and MyAdvisor

Executive Summary

In 2016, Royal Bank of Canada (RBC) launched its first native mobile app. At that time, despite being the largest bank in Canada, RBC was ranked 'seventh of the big five banks' in Canada digitally, particularly for mobile banking. To close this significant gap, it had to make significant investments in mobile and more broadly in digital banking.

Over the past five years RBC has been transforming the bank's five business lines to ensure digital relevance, while also focusing on building an agile culture to compete with more nimble emerging competitors like big tech and platform players. They have changed how they work, moving from waterfall to agile. The bank has adopted design thinking and continuous client and advisor feedback, by doubling down on the partnership between business and technology. They deliver value through frequent iterations, which increases speed to market and reduces risk, fail fast, fail small.

Moving to a single stack infrastructure has also helped RBC structure its transformation around customer journeys and by building reusable components for both advisors and clients they can scale across all channels. This strategic approach centred around customer journeys and the introduction of agile has fundamentally shifted the cadence of the bank, from bi-monthly releases to 7–12 releases a day underpinned by over 100 agile squads working on mid-tier services, browser and native client experiences.

Since its launch in August 2017, NOMI clients have reviewed more than 1.5 billion insights, increased their dwell time on the mobile banking app and given the bank a net promoter score (NPS) of 86.5+. So far 2.35 million Canadians have created a personalised financial plan using MyAdvisor.

Introductions

Do you want more details about this case? Find additional highlights from these interviews at www.howbanksinnovate.com.

Peter Tilton, Senior Vice President, Digital

Peter joined RBC in 2016 as the Senior Vice President of Digital, Personal and Commercial Banking. In this role Peter leads RBC's shift to a more technology-enabled, digitally driven bank. He is responsible for identifying and capitalising on ways to leverage digital to further position RBC as a global leader in digital banking. Peter has oversight of building the framework to drive the convergence of digital channels with sales, service and contact center platforms. Peter is also responsible for direct client experiences across mobile, online, tablet and wearables, including banking, direct investing, wallet and rewards solutions. Prior to RBC, Peter was Head of Digital Banking for Australia and New Zealand Banking Group Ltd (ANZ Bank). Peter has a Computer Science and Education Degree from the University of Melbourne and his Master's in Human Resources Development from Queensland University of Technology.

Sumit Oberai, Senior Vice President, Digital Technology

Sumit is Senior Vice President, Digital Technology at RBC, where he helps to drive RBC's shift to a more technology-enabled, digitally driven bank. He co-leads the Digital organisation with responsibility for online banking, mobile banking, loyalty and rewards, online brokerage, digital payments and new digital product launches. He also has responsibility for RBC's API strategy, both as an internal 'mid-tier' and externally in the form of an API store enabling partnerships and business model extensions. As a member of RBC's Technology and Operations (T&O) Operating Committee, he contributes to the development of the overall strategy and direction of T&O.

Sumit began his career as a software developer at Nortel Networks. Prior to joining RBC in 2016, Sumit spent 10 years at Indigo Books and Music. His last role was Chief Information Officer and Executive Vice President of Loyalty, where he was responsible for all technology functions as well as Indigo's loyalty and customer intelligence programmes. Prior to Indigo, Sumit led engineering organisations at venture-backed companies, DocSpace and Eloqua, which each were acquired for over $500 million CAD, and he also worked as a consultant for McKinsey and Company. He also sat on Visa Canada's Advisory Board.

Sumit holds an MBA from INSEAD in France, an MEng in Computer Engineering from the University of Toronto and a BEng in Mathematics and Engineering from Queens University.

Sumit lives in Toronto with his wife, Marcia, and their three children.

Rami Thabet, Vice President, Digital Product

Rami is the Vice President of Digital Product. In this role Rami leads the team responsible for the envisioning, building and shipping industry leading digital products. He is responsible for RBC's digital channels, omnichannel experiences and key capabilities, such as identity and security and the API platform.

Rami has been with RBC for over seven years and held various roles in Marketing and Channel Strategy, Technology and Operations, Payments and Cards and Digital. Most recently, Rami led the mobile, tablet and wearables organisation and delivered on a number of key capabilities and Canadian firsts in payments, identity and the NOMI Artificial Intelligence platform, as well as the creation of RBC's J.D. Power award-winning mobile platform. His team has recently been awarded the Celent's Model Bank of the Year award for delivering personalized client engagement, creating exceptional customer-focused experiences and building digital literacy among employees.

Prior to his time at RBC, Rami held a number of roles across business, technology and consulting in the financial, technology and public sectors, including BMO, CIBC, Manulife, Cancer Care Ontario, Ontario Government and CGI.

Rami graduated from Harvard University with a BA in Mathematics and Artificial Intelligence. He also holds an MBA from Cornell University.

Background

Key Figures

Total assets: C$1.6 trillion
Number of customers: 17 million
Number of branches: 1,200
Number of full-time employees: 86,000
(Approximate as of 2020)

The Royal Bank of Canada (RBC) is Canada's largest bank by market capitalization. RBC provides personal and commercial banking, wealth management services, insurance, investor services, and capital markets products and services on a global basis. It serves personal, business, public sector, and institutional clients through offices in Canada, the United States and 34 other countries.

It was the first bank in Canada to perform a financial transaction, the first with a website and a global pioneer for digital wallets. RBC was the first Canadian bank to launch a public API developer portal in 2018 and the first to deliver AI-powered insights at scale.

Digital at RBC consists of both business and technology teams under joint leadership. The team contains Digital Product and Business Analysis, Strategy, Design and Operations on the Business side and Delivery, Development, Architecture and Quality Engineering on the Technology side. Teams work collaboratively in cross-functional customer journeys with squads co-located to ensure maximum productivity. The Digital Team develops on a single omnichannel software stack for all retail and commercial customers and advisors. This means that RBC can build once and deliver both to the relevant front-line employees and directly to customers.

Problem

'We needed to increase our aperture, the lens with which we talked about the art of the possible. Fear of failure is normal, but we wanted to overcome that with excitement about what is next.'

Rami Thabet, Vice President, Digital Product

In 2016, it launched its first native mobile app. At that time, despite being the largest bank in Canada, RBC was ranked 'seventh of the big five banks' in Canada digitally, particularly for mobile banking. To close this gap, it had to make significant investments in mobile and more broadly in digital banking.

A new way of working would be needed to increase speed to market and to stay ahead of competition. Client expectations are still rapidly changing at a time when banks are increasingly being compared to non-traditional competitors like big tech firms. As consumer interest in digital banking solutions grew, their confidence in using them also grew. The bank's technology infrastructure was inflexible and consisted of several different platforms across the bank. This meant that solutions delivered were creating inconsistent client and staff experiences, as well as slowing solution releases and upgrades. RBC were spending too much time prioritising and funding hundreds of small projects for what felt like incremental gains.

To make this possible, in 2017 the bank made the decision to build a new omnichannel platform. It is a common technology for clients and advisors that spans card-only consumers to personal retail to corporate, across mobile, online and in branch. Having digitised everyday banking and simple sales, like payments, balances, insights, nudges and self-managed account opening, the bank is now focusing on the digitisation of relationship and advice, in both cases of automated and advisor-led experiences.

RBC has structured its transformation around building reusable components for both advisors and clients so that they can scale across all channels. This strategic approach centred around customer journeys and the introduction of agile procedures has fundamentally shifted the cadence of the bank, moving from bi-monthly releases to 7–12 releases a day underpinned by over 100 agile squads working on mid-tier services, browser and native client experiences.

How could it capture greater business benefits from its digital channels, defend its market position against existing and non-traditional competitors, and manage a massive digital transformation at the same time?

Solution

'Before we had to push and fight for more digital innovation, but now we have reached a point where innovation is self-perpetual, everyone sees the value it creates.'

Peter Tilton, Senior Vice President, Digital

Like many other FIs, RBC started digitising the simple transactions because its clients wanted convenient banking solutions. As clients became more comfortable banking digitally, they started to want to do more complex banking. RBC discovered the need for advice, and subsequently its advisors were still just as much in demand. It began to see a ceiling emerge in terms of the value that clients and the bank were getting from digital.

The biggest step for RBC was to bring this advice services online and into the homes and palms of clients while still focusing on compelling user experiences. It would require significant investment to digitise the core of the bank and the way it delivers advice.

As you move along the spectrum from digitising transactions to digitising advice, the book value of digital solutions increases as clients complete more complex transactions, like corporate credit and home lending. It also is where there is an opportunity to streamline complex operational processes with straight-through processing, helping drive down cost and time to serve. In addition to the direct business benefits, the complexity of the challenge may have also been what was so attractive for RBC. Given their scale and size, if they could get this right, the bank believed it could be at a significant competitive advantage, one that would be very difficult for a fintech or smaller bank to replicate.

RBC classifies advice as either (a) digitally driven or (b) digitally enabled, human-led. Digitally driven advice is about leveraging AI, data and analytics to deliver insights and nudges that provide clients with a useful banking experience that makes them feel in control of their finances. This ecosystem is automated and self-serve in nature and can help people budget, manage their cash flow and create personalised experiences. Digitally enabled, human-led advice leverages technology to enable their advisors and clients to connect, regardless of where they are.

An example of digitally driven advice was the launch of NOMI. NOMI Insights helps clients manage their everyday finances by providing timely and personalised trends, alerts and overviews based on spending and saving habits. NOMI Budgets helps clients by taking the thinking, and the manual calculator work, out of setting up a budget. It takes a close look at a client's spending and recommends a personalized monthly budget based on their habits. Since its launch in April 2019, more than one million clients have set more than 1,700,000 budgets. NOMI Find & Save uses predictive technology to find money that clients can spare and automatically sets it aside for them. Clients using this feature have found on average about $350/month, adding up to about $4,200 per year.

RBC is now developing new AI technology to augment various pieces of the digital consumer experience, like personalised servicing experiences and AI-powered money management. Long short-term memory (LSTM) methods for time series forecasting are being researched as a technology to help clients understand their upcoming financial obligations. Improving a client's financial efficacy means they can make better plans and decisions regarding their future financial goals. Personalised digital servicing features and experiences are also under development. For example, a digital experience that anticipates clients' needs, then optimises their digital fulfillment, such as predicting key upcoming banking needs like an upcoming payment or financial commitment, can enable

RBC to adapt an existing digital experience and deepen engagement and satisfaction.

An example of digitally enabled, human-led advice is the introduction of MyAdvisor. Launched in 2017, MyAdvisor is a solution that connects a client with an advisor through live video, phone or in-person and together they can create a digital, personalised plan that is dynamic and always available to the client through RBC online banking. The bank also expanded the platform to support a wider group of advisors, including those within Private Banking.

Delivery

'A few years ago, 80% of our talent came from other financial institutions, today that number is only 20%. We are hiring talent regardless of their background to ensure we are as diverse as our customers.'

Sumit Oberai, Senior Vice President, Digital Technology

Over the past five years RBC has been transforming the bank's five business lines to ensure digital relevance, while also focusing on building an agile culture to compete with more nimble emerging competitors like big tech and platform players. They have changed how they work, moving from waterfall to agile. The bank has adopted design thinking and continuous client and advisor feedback, by doubling down on the partnership between business and technology. They deliver value through frequent iterations, which increases speed to market and reduces risk, fail fast, fail small. One way they do this is with a model branch, a branch where the advisors have agreed to be product testers for the digital team, providing both the client and their feedback on the tools built.

From a technology perspective, the largest transformation RBC undertook was aligning their digital platforms on a single modern technology stack. They invested in an omnichannel platform that can deliver seamless experiences for clients and advisors regardless of when, where and how they want to connect with the bank. Today a client can traverse from mobile to talking to someone in a branch or having a video conference with an advisor all in a seamless digital experience.

The move to adopt modular, flexible architecture also provided the bank with the ability to increase their speed to market as it allows them to reuse and scale rapidly. Part of this process was getting business and technology heads to understand the value of building shared components, shared platforms, share systems and reusability, instead of trying to individually fund and develop every product or channel on separate platforms. Crossing several different businesses in the bank has not been easy for the bank.

One way RBC has been able to do this has been by aligning digital resources under one horizontal team to cross the bank's virtual business lines. Digital product, design, operations and technology teams are even physically collocated and work in lockstep. It helps to visualise an end-to-end banking experience through both a customer and advisor lens to solve problems that delight and deepen relationships. Customer journeys span multiple interactions and channels, and enable cross-functional teams to collaborate and build seamless experiences for both clients and employees.

The closer collaboration is also a powerful way to break down organisational silos and reduce the burden of traditional project prioritisation and funding, since they are most effectively delivered through a continuously funded agile operating model.

Results

Since its launch in August 2017, NOMI clients have reviewed more than 1.5 billion insights, increased their dwell time on the mobile banking app and given the bank an NPS of 86.5+. So far more than two million Canadians have created a personalised financial plan using MyAdvisor.

Moving to a single stack infrastructure has also helped RBC structure its transformation around customer journeys and by building reusable components for both advisors and clients they can scale across all channels. This strategic approach centred around customer journeys and the introduction of agile has fundamentally shifted the cadence of the bank, from bi-monthly releases to 7–12 releases a day underpinned by over 100 agile squads working on mid-tier services, browser and native client experiences.

It also increased RBC's speed to market as it allows them to reuse and scale rapidly, moving towards modular, flexible architecture for faster time to market and more flexibility. Equally important, it helps find efficiency, captures benefits from back office activities by automating them and drives straight-through processing to deliver solutions faster.

Learnings

In terms of learnings, Peter and Sumit shared the following:

For Peter, three things he would have done differently included:

- Invest more to scale up the agile practice with greater pace. We are a conservative bank and tested and refined our way through. However, if starting now it would be possible to onboard talent more quickly and grow at least 30–40% more rapidly with similar quality outcomes.
- Focus earlier on defining, road-mapping and building re-usable patterns and components.
- Align the broader organisation into the digital practice earlier.

For Sumit:

- To make agile successful, ensure you have the right internal leadership (on the ground and senior leadership support) and get external help where needed. RBC has had false starts on shifting to a scaled agile software development practice in the past without these conditions being met. A regular senior 'roadblock elimination' forum (versus a 'steering committee') helped drive the right mindset and behaviours.

- As success starts to build, start to extend the footprint to drive to end impact (e.g. with core systems, operations teams) to grow the value unlocked.
- Be willing to invest in horizontal teams that drive effectiveness of the overall programme (e.g. platform engineering or design and product practice experts).

What's Next

With a focused effort, RBC believes it could reach 98% in digital self-serve transactions and a digital sales mix of about 50%. However, even with that, RBC estimates that digitising simple transactions can only address about 30% of the bank's costs and only win about 10% of the bank's revenue.

Having successfully digitised everyday banking and simple sales, like payments, balances, insights, nudges and self-managed account opening, the bank is now focusing on further digitisation of relationship and advice, in both cases of automated and advisor-led experiences.

Index